Learning to Live for God

Learning to Live for God

C. D. Maire

EVANGELICAL PRESS

EVANGELICAL PRESS
P.O. Box 5, Welwyn, Hertfordshire, AL6 9NU, England

First published in French under the title
Connaître Dieu pour mieux le servir
First English edition 1979
© Evangelical Press 1979

ISBN 0 85234 132 6

Cover design by Peter Wagstaff

Typeset by Computacomp (UK) Ltd, Fort William, Scotland
Printed in Great Britain by Billing & Sons Ltd., Guildford, London and
Worcester

Contents

Foreword

True Christianity is not simply believing a creed of
doctrine or observing certain religious practices. It
involves a knowledge of God and ourselves, and a true
and sincere obedience to God. In this book the author,
Charles-Daniel Maire, treats both these aspects of
Christianity.

This is not a deep theological work or an academic
study of Christian doctrine. It is a simple explanation of
the biblical teaching on the major doctrines of the
Christian faith and a straightforward application to
everyday life. No attempt has been made to deal with
complicated issues which give rise to differences of
opinion among evangelical Christians and which could
confuse the reader for whom this book is intended.

The book is based on a series of studies which were
originally broadcast over Radio ELWA in West Africa. It
is therefore particularly adapted for Africa and Third
World Countries, although the basic teaching has world-
wide relevance.

There are three sections in the book. The first sets out
some great doctrines of the Bible, the second explains
how to become a Christian, and the third gives practical
guidance on how to live the Christian life. One of the
important features is the appendix which contains
lessons and questions for further study. The book is
therefore especially suitable for use as a manual for
senior Sunday School or Bible study classes.

Major quotations from the Bible have been printed in
full for easier reading. These quotations are from the
New American Standard Version. Other Scripture
references given in the text will enable the reader to study
further the points raised.

The Publishers

Part 1 The major doctrines

Introduction

What is a doctrine?

A doctrine is a teaching given by a master who is recognized as having authority (Matthew 7:28-29). It is also the whole of the Bible's teaching on any one subject. For example, by bringing together all that the Bible says about man we arrive at the biblical doctrine of man. By Christian doctrine we mean the sum total of the individual biblical doctrines.

A word of warning

Let us not mix our own ideas, or doctrines invented by men, with what the Bible says (Hebrews 13:9; 1 Timothy 1:3). Neither must we establish a doctrine by basing it on a personal experience, however decisive the experience may have been in our own lives. In this first part we shall study the most important biblical doctrines, those which constitute basic Christian doctrine.

1
Revelation

Can we know God?

All the religions of the world are efforts by man to lift himself up to God. Short of reaching God Himself, most of them teach that we should serve intermediary beings: spirits, the sun, the moon, etc. ... The Bible, on the other hand, teaches us that God has made Himself known. It even declares that it is possible to know Him personally. How can the great God, the Creator of heaven and earth, the great invisible and infinite God—how can He speak to us? That is what we are going to study in this first chapter. This act by which God has made Himself known is called *revelation*.

Natural revelation

Nature is a vast book which speaks to us about God. The apostle Paul writes, 'Since the creation of the world His invisible attributes, His eternal power and divine nature, have been clearly seen, being understood through what has been made ...' (Romans 1:20).

When we look at a work of art, we admire the artist's talent. Faced with the wonders of nature, contemplating the power of the waves of the sea or the splendour of a sunset, we have to exclaim with David, 'The heavens are telling of the glory of God; and their expanse is declaring the work of His hands' (Psalm 19:1).

This revelation is so clear that those who turn away from God are without excuse; but it is insufficient to explain to us *all* that God wants to tell us for our salvation. That is why God has used other means as well.

Spoken revelation

God often commands that the words He addresses to His servants should be written down in a book (Revelation 1:11; Exodus 17:14; Isaiah 8:1). These books were written by a large number of authors, the first of whom was, no doubt, Moses. These men, who were chosen by God to write down His Word, also gathered together documents relating to their ancestors. They were guided in this difficult work by the Holy Spirit of God who revealed to them what no human tradition could have taught them. The sixty-six books of the Bible teach us to know God chiefly because they all speak to us about Jesus Christ (John 5:39). The Old Testament foretells His coming, the New Testament tells the story of His life, death and resurrection, and explains how His work brings salvation. Remember that the word 'testament' comes from a Latin word meaning 'covenant'. The Old Testament is the book of the Old Covenant, the covenant which God had made with the people of Israel before the coming of Jesus Christ. The New Testament is the book of the New Covenant made by Jesus Christ.

Revelation in Jesus Christ

The whole Bible bears witness to Jesus Christ, the great revelation which surpasses all others. The author of the Epistle to the Hebrews declares, 'God, after He spoke long ago to the fathers in the prophets in many portions and in many ways, in these last days has spoken to us in His Son' (Hebrews 1:1–2).

In Jesus Christ, God became man; He has spoken to us directly through His mouth and through all His acts. The apostle John writes, 'The Word was God' (John 1:1). Later he adds: 'The Word became flesh, and dwelt among us, and we beheld His glory, glory as of the only begotten from the Father, full of grace and truth' (John 1:14).

In Jesus Christ, God has come to meet us. We cannot

understand how the great God of heaven was able to
stoop down to our level, but it is a fact (Philippians 2:5–9).
It is the Bible, the written revelation, which tells us how
this happened. But how do we know that the Bible tells us
the truth?

The authority of the Bible

The inspiration of the Bible

The word 'Bible' means 'book'. However, the Bible is not
just a book like any other, but is in a class by itself. It was
inspired by God. 'All Scripture is inspired by God'
(2 Timothy 3:16).

What do we mean by the inspiration of the Bible? God
could easily have made a book fall out of the sky, already
written. But He chose to use men with their own
characters, gifts, ways of thinking and language.
However, the Bible was not written by men alone. God
made them able to write it, by putting His Word in their
heart (2 Peter 1:21). To inspire means to 'breathe into'.
By His Spirit, therefore, God breathed His Word into the
heart of His servants.

The Bible is the Word of God

The Bible claims to be the Word of God. The Old
Testament prophets often prefaced what they said with
such words as: 'For thus the Lord spoke to me ...' (Isaiah
8:11); 'And the word of the Lord came to me ...'
(Jeremiah 1:11).

The men who wrote the New Testament were also
aware that their message was the very Word of God. Paul
declares, 'When you received from us the word of God's
message, you accepted it not as the word of men, but for
what it really is, the word of God, which also performs its
work in you who believe' (1 Thessalonians 2:13).

Unless we are going to accuse Isaiah, Jeremiah and Paul
of deliberately deceiving their readers, we have to

recognize with them that their writings are indeed the Word of God.

The Word of God is truth

Jesus Himself declared, 'Thy word is truth' (John 17:17).

We can never have absolute confidence in what men say, but, because it is the Word of God, we can have absolute confidence in the Bible (Titus 1:2). In everything that concerns faith in God, the moral conduct of men, and eternity, the Bible is the only source of knowledge.

Because the Bible is the Word of God, it has great authority; because it has been written by men, in human language, we can understand it.

Science and the Bible

We hear it said that science and the Bible contradict each other. Some people even affirm that it is no longer possible to believe in the Bible since man has made certain great scientific discoveries. We should not allow ourselves to be influenced by statements of this sort, because they are founded on a lack of information or on the desire to undermine the authority of the Bible. The Holy Scriptures tell us about things which science will never be able to discover or explain. They teach us that the world was created by God and for God. The Bible also tells us how God has made Himself known all down the history of mankind.

It is true that the Bible was not set out in the style of a modern scientific treatise, but it was written in such a way as to be understood by all men, in all ages. The Bible is therefore still God's letter to lost humanity. The role of science is to discover and explain the hidden things of nature and not to try to replace God and His Word by human ideas, which is only a new form of idolatry.

2
The doctrine of God

A word of warning

It is difficult to study this doctrine. If we try to understand things which are beyond us, we run the risk of distorting biblical revelation. Can a tree, which has no eyes or ears, know what man is like? If the tree could speak, it would say that man has branches! It would probably find it very difficult to understand that man has no roots for getting food from the ground! The tree cannot imagine man. And even less can man have any conception of the great God of heaven. That is why God forbids us in His Word to portray Him visually (Exodus 20:4). Therefore our attitude as we learn to know our Creator and Saviour must be one of humility, prayerfulness, adoration and submission to Holy Scripture.

There is only one God

The Old and New Testaments both declare that there is only one God. 'Hear, O Israel! The Lord is our God, the Lord is one!' (Deuteronomy 6:4). 'You believe that God is one. You do well' (James 2:19). (See also Malachi 2:10; 1 Kings 8:60; 1 Timothy 2:5.)

Most traditional African religions teach that there is only one Creator God. But according to them, God, the Creator, is far away from us. That is why these religions are not very concerned with Him. They recommend that we concentrate on serving secondary gods. The Bible teaches clearly that there are no other gods. Only the Lord God, the Creator, is to be served (Exodus 20:3).

The mystery of the Trinity

The word 'trinity' is not in the Bible, but it was invented to express a biblical truth. The one and only God is so great, so far beyond us, that He is at the same time 'Father, Son and Holy Spirit, one God blessed for ever'. Christians have sometimes been accused of worshipping three Gods. This is a misunderstanding. Christians worship only one God, but this one God is in three Persons. In fact when the Bible speaks to us about God it sometimes specifies God the Father, sometimes God the Son and sometimes God the Holy Spirit.

God the Father

'Thou, O Lord, art our Father' (Isaiah 63:16). Jesus said to Mary Magdalene, 'I ascend to My Father and your Father, and My God and your God' (John 20:17).

God the Son

'For a child will be born to us, a son will be given to us' (Isaiah 9:6). At His baptism Jesus heard these words from heaven: 'This is My beloved Son ...' (Matthew 3:17).

God the Holy Spirit

'The Spirit of God has made me, and the breath of the Almighty gives me life' (Job 33:4). The apostle Paul urged the Ephesians, 'Do not grieve the Holy Spirit of God' (Ephesians 4:30).

We are quite certain that there are three distinct Persons, since the three are mentioned together in several texts: 'Go therefore and make disciples of all the nations, baptizing them in the name of the Father and the Son and the Holy Spirit' (Matthew 28:19). 'The grace of the Lord Jesus Christ, and the love of God, and the fellowship of the Holy Spirit, be with you all' (2 Corinthians 13:14).

When we say that God is in three Persons, we must not give the word 'person' its usual sense. God is not a limited human being. The highest heavens cannot contain Him (1 Kings 8:27). How can human words describe what is beyond the imagination of human thought?

The comparison between the tree and the man can help us again here. A tree is a simple creature. You can cut off its branches and it is still a tree. Man is far more complex. There is such a close connection between all his members that you have only to tear off an arm or a hand to put his life in danger, and a man with no heart or no head is no longer a man. God is infinitely more difficult to understand than man. He is not made up of parts like a human being, but of three Persons joined together like the parts of a body to form one single Being. Just as a man cannot exist without a heart or a head, in the same way, God would no longer be the God of the Bible without the Son and without the Holy Spirit.

The Trinity and the experience of salvation

Even the Christian who does not yet have a deep knowledge of this doctrine knows that the Father has created him and loved him (John 3:16). He knows that Jesus Christ the Son has died for him (Romans 3:25). He knows too that the Holy Spirit has given him a new life.

Before examining in more detail the doctrine of the Son and of the Holy Spirit, we need to review a few more teachings about God. We shall therefore spend a little longer considering the Father, the Son and the Holy Spirit. However, any one of the following points may also be applied to one particular Person in the Trinity.

God is eternal

The word 'eternal' means, 'having neither beginning nor

end' (Psalm 90:2–4; Hebrews 1:12). God is always the same; speaking to Moses, He said, 'I am who I am; ... thus you shall say to the sons of Israel, "I Am has sent me to you"' (Exodus 3:14).

His love and His justice remain forever. He is unchanging (Malachi 3:6; James 1:17). In our world where everything changes, it is a precious thing to be able to put our trust in a God who does not change.

God is all-powerful

God is often called the all-powerful One. That means that He can do all things: 'But our God is in the heavens; He does whatever He pleases' (Psalm 115:3). Jesus said to His disciples, 'With God all things are possible' (Matthew 19:26). He is Sovereign, King and Lord.

Satan, the enemy of God, can appear to be very powerful. He is even called the prince of this world. However, his power is limited by God (Job 1:12; Job 2:6). Men think that they are free to do what they want, but in fact, in spite of themselves, they are carrying out God's plans. This is very difficult to understand. The death of Jesus is an example of this mystery. The men who condemned Him were accomplishing the greatest evil of all time, but in His grace, God brought out of this great evil the greatest possible good which He could do for men. He gave them salvation and eternal life.

In His omnipotence and His infinite love, God knows how to bring good out of evil. The story of Joseph illustrates this truth (Genesis 37–47). Joseph was sold as a slave by his brothers, but several years later, he became the Prime Minister of Egypt, and by this fact, saved his brothers. Were Joseph's brothers less guilty of that? No. Those who do evil are fully responsible. But God, who is above, remains the all-powerful Master. It is a great encouragement that we can rely on a God who can do all things.

God is everywhere

A proverb says, 'God can see the black ant, on a black stone, on the blackest night!' This is quite true. King David expresses this truth in this way:

'Where can I go from Thy Spirit?
Or where can I flee from Thy presence?
If I ascend to heaven, Thou art there;
If I make my bed in Sheol, behold, Thou art there.
If I take the wings of the dawn,
If I dwell in the remotest part of the sea,
Even there Thy hand will lead me,
And Thy right hand will lay hold of me.
If I say, "Surely the darkness will overwhelm me,
And the light around me will be night,"
Even the darkness is not dark to Thee,
And the night is as bright as the day.
Darkness and light are alike to Thee' (Psalm 139:7–12).

Because God is everywhere, He sees everything. Because He sees everything He can be perfectly just in His judgements (Proverbs 15:3). The knowledge of this startling truth should drive us to repent and make us conscientious and honest in everything that we undertake.

God knows everything

God knows everything because He sees everything (1 John 3:20). He knows even our most secret thoughts:

'O Lord, Thou hast searched me and known me.
Thou dost know when I sit down and when I rise up;
Thou dost understand my thought from afar.
Thou dost scrutinize my path and my lying down,
And art intimately acquainted with all my ways.
Even before there is a word on my tongue,
Behold, O Lord, Thou dost know it all' (Psalm 139:1–4).

God knows the past; the future has no secrets for Him.

He knows everything in advance. Therefore He can guide us, leading us by the best road (Psalm 139:16). Because we are sure that He knows everything, we can leave the direction of our lives to Him.

God is love

African religions also teach that God, the Creator, is everywhere and that He will judge men. But they never speak of a God of love who is the Father of those who serve Him. But what is this love of God?

First of all, God's love does not count the cost; He gives freely His most precious possession: 'For God so loved the world, that He gave His only begotten Son, that whoever believes in Him should not perish, but have eternal life' (John 3:16).

Secondly, because of His love, God has taken the initiative in our salvation; He offers us His grace, even before we ask Him for it: 'We love because He first loved us' (1 John 4:19, see also Romans 5:8).

Thirdly, our Lord rejoices each time a sinner repents. This is not a love which acts out of duty, because it is obliged to do so, on the contrary, God finds joy in saving us. The parable of the two sons illustrates this truth (Luke 15:11–32).

Finally, the love of God lasts forever (Romans 8:37–39). He will never forsake us (Psalm 136).

'If we are faithless, He remains faithful; for He cannot deny Himself' (2 Timothy 2:13).

The Bible often speaks of God's 'mercy'. This word speaks to us of the love of God. God has compassion on our hopelessness. It is also because of His love that God is patient, that He does not punish us immediately, but allows us time to return to Him (2 Peter 3:9).

God is just

The justice of God is not simply His quality of being a just

Judge (2 Timothy 4:8), but the guarantee that all that God does is perfect. He has nothing at all with which to reproach Himself. Men do not understand this justice. Faced with the mystery of death, or of the suffering of innocent people, we sometimes find ourselves asking, 'Why does God permit it?' At such times, let us remember these words of Jeremiah: 'Righteous art Thou, O Lord, that I would plead my case with Thee' (Jeremiah 12:1).

We do not always understand God's justice, but we are absolutely overwhelmed when God makes us a gift of His righteousness in Jesus Christ. 'All have sinned and fall short of the glory of God, being justified as a gift by His grace through the redemption which is in Christ Jesus' (Romans 3:23–24).

God is holy

'I am the Lord your God. ... Be holy; for I am holy' (Leviticus 11:44). The word 'holy' means 'separate from evil'. God's holiness is the result of His love and His justice. Evil, in fact, is always opposed to love and justice. The prophet Habakkuk exclaimed, 'Thine eyes are too pure to approve evil, and Thou canst not look on wickedness with favour' (Habakkuk 1:13).

That is why God cannot accept sinful man. It is because of God's holiness that our sin must be covered by the blood of Jesus Christ.

Meditation on the doctrine of God cannot leave us unmoved; the knowledge of God should transform us. The Bible tells us 'God is love'; it adds, 'You shall love' (Deuteronomy 6:5). God is just; the Bible commands, 'Do justice' (Micah 6:8). God is holy, the Bible commands, 'Be holy' (1 Peter 1:15).

Let us bow before the greatness of the Lord, and walk in His ways, in the joy of His presence.

3

The doctrine of the Son

The importance of this doctrine

It is through Jesus Christ that God has made Himself
known. It is in Him that we must believe if we are to be
saved. But to believe in Him, we must know who He is.
Jesus Christ is also the Christian's pattern. Before we can
learn to live as He did, we must know Him well.
Therefore, in this chapter we shall study what the Bible
says about His person, His life and His work. It is love that
caused God to reveal Himself in Jesus Christ; so let us
learn to know Him, as we in our turn, are motivated by
love for the One who has saved us.

The person of Jesus Christ

The names the Bible gives to Jesus Christ

For the Jews as for Africans, a person's name is very
important. The name tells us precisely who the person is.
The study of the names given to the Saviour is therefore
full of valuable instruction about His person.

Jesus

This name comes from Hebrew, the language of the
Jews. It means 'God saves' (Matthew 1:21).

Christ

This name comes from Greek, the language used by
the writers of the New Testament. It is the translation
of the Hebrew word *maschiach*, which means 'anointed'.

This Hebrew word has given us the English word 'Messiah'. According to the custom of the people of Israel, men who were chosen to be prophet, priest or king were anointed with oil. This very old custom was practised to show that the prophets, priests or kings were not chosen by men, but by God.

Jesus truly is the Christ, the Messiah, because He was chosen to minister in each of these three ways.

Prophet

Jesus speaks on behalf of God. His teaching occupies a very large place in His ministry (Deuteronomy 18:15).

Priest

He offered the one great sacrifice, which was sufficient to atone for the sins of all men (Hebrews 8:1–2).

King

Jesus has received all power from His Father. He is the successor who was promised to David. His reign has no end (Matthew 21:5).

Son of Man

By this title, the Bible teaches that Jesus is really man. But Jesus is not just any man. He is without sin. Therefore He can offer Himself to God for all men (1 Peter 2:22; 2 Corinthians 5:21; Hebrews 2:17).

Son of God

There is something slightly shocking about this title. Indeed, how can God have a Son? In the Bible this expression is not being used in its usual sense. It never means that the Son of God was born from the union of God with a woman. The Son of God is eternal. He has neither beginning nor end. He became the Son of Man by

His birth at Bethlehem; but He has *always* been the Son of God. He Himself said, 'Before Abraham was born, I Am' (John 8:58).

It is impossible for us to understand how the Son of God became man in Jesus Christ, but we can grasp why this miracle was necessary for our salvation. The story is told of a man who, while out walking in the bush, discovered an anthill which had been half destroyed by some animal. Moved by the sight of these wounded ants, the man bent down. He tried to help them. But the more he tried to help them, the more he found he was crushing the poor ants. His fingers were too big. Then he began to think. He soon understood what he would have to do, but it was impossible. He, the big man, would have to become an ant. If he were as small as an ant and as strong as a man, he would be able to help them. This is exactly what God does. As Son of God, Jesus is really God. His sacrifice is capable of blotting out the sins of all men. As Son of Man, Jesus is really man. He is one of us. Therefore, He was able to take our guilt upon Himself, and to bear in our place the punishment which we deserved (Romans 9:5; John 20:28; Matthew 1:23).

The life of Jesus Christ

The birth of Jesus

Jesus' birth was miraculous. His mother Mary brought Him into the world without the help of any man. The angel said to Joseph, who was engaged to Mary, 'That which has been conceived in her is of the Holy Spirit' (Matthew 1:20).

Born of a woman, Jesus is truly a man. But the miracle of His conception is evidence that He is truly God.

The birth of Jesus is a historical fact. Even unbelievers count the years from the date of His birth. It was during the reign of a well-known emperor, Caesar Augustus, that Jesus was born 'in the days of Herod the king' (Luke

2:1; Matthew 2:1). All Jews know about this king because of his cruelty.

From the moment of His birth, Jesus experienced intense suffering. He was born in a cowshed, because no one would take Him in. Only a few shepherds and the mysterious magi came to worship Him. King Herod, jealous and bloodthirsty, wanted to kill Him. Mary and Joseph had to flee to Egypt to save His life. His birth foreshadowed His life and His death. Indeed, from the very beginning of His life on earth, He took upon Himself our misery and endured human wickedness.

The baptism of Jesus

Jesus was without sin. He did not therefore need to be baptized with the baptism of repentance. However, He told the amazed John the Baptist, 'Permit it at this time; for in this way it is fitting for us to fulfil all righteousness' (Matthew 3:15).

By being baptized, even though He did not need to be, since He was without sin, Jesus showed officially what He had come to do on earth. He went down into the water into which many sinners had gone before Him to be baptized. This striking gesture was to show better than words could do that Jesus came to take upon Himself the sin of mankind. He therefore also received the punishment instead of them.

The story is told of a murderer wanted by the police. The assassin fled to his home and exchanged his clothes with his brother. The innocent brother, dressed in the blood-stained clothes of the guilty one, was arrested, imprisoned and condemned. This is what Jesus did at His baptism. He took our sin upon Him, to carry it until His death. When we are baptized, we declare that we leave in the water the filthy rags of our sin and receive the white robe of Jesus Christ's righteousness.

The temptation of Jesus

It is the hard battles which show who are the great

champions. The more victories they win over formidable enemies, the more they show their strength. Jesus was God's champion. After having fasted for forty days and forty nights, He met His worst enemy, Satan, face to face! This adversary attacked Jesus in the most cunning fashion possible, using words taken from the Bible to tempt the Son of God. Not only did Jesus not fall, but He put His opponent to flight. This glorious victory shows that Jesus is really able to give the victory to those who put their trust in Him, when they are tempted (Matthew 4:1–11; Luke 4:1–13; Hebrews 2:18).

The miracles of Jesus

During His three years of ministry Jesus, accompanied by His disciples, travelled incessantly. He visited all parts of His country, and sometimes even went outside the land of Israel (Matthew 15:21). He drew immense crowds. The sick, the blind, those who were paralysed and who were possessed by evil spirits were brought to Him. Jesus performed very many miracles (John 12:37; John 20:30). The crowds were so impressed that many believed in Him (John 2:23). Jesus performed His miracles because of His love for people who were in trouble. This fact teaches us that He came to earth really to help us. His miracles also show clearly that He is not simply a man. Nicodemus said to Jesus, 'No one can do these signs that You do unless God is with him' (John 3:2).

Later the disciples also performed miracles but they did so *in the name of Jesus* (Acts 3:6). The miracles are therefore a proof of His deity.

The teaching of Jesus

Jesus gave several long talks. In the first of these, which is known as the sermon on the mount, Jesus declared plainly that He did not come to abolish the Old Testament Law, but to fulfil it. Most of what He said explained the way in which His followers must also fulfil the Law of God. Jesus summed up the Law and all its teaching in these words: 'You shall love the Lord your God with all your heart, and with all your soul, and with all your mind. This is the great and foremost commandment. And a second is like it, you shall love your neighbour as yourself' (Matthew 22:37–39).

Jesus also announced the coming of the kingdom of heaven, or the kingdom of God (Matthew 13). This kingdom is a hidden power, the presence of God which manifests itself in the heart and life of true disciples.

Jesus met with more and more opposition. So He began to speak in parables. A parable is a spiritual truth hidden in a story about everyday life. This is the way Jesus teaches those whose hearts are sincere. But His enemies cannot discover the truth intended for the true disciples (Matthew 13:10–17).

The condemnation of Jesus

The more He taught, and the more miracles He performed, the more Jesus' enemies opposed Him. The Jewish religious leaders hated Jesus. They wanted to be rid of Him. After three years of ministry, Jesus went up to Jerusalem, according to the Jewish custom, to celebrate the Passover (Matthew 20:17). This feast reminded the children of Israel of their deliverance from Egypt where they had been slaves. A week before the festival, Jesus was hailed by the crowd who shouted, 'Hosanna to the Son of David; blessed is He who comes in the name of the Lord; hosanna in the highest!' (Matthew 21:9).

But Jesus had hardly entered Jerusalem, when He drove the money-lenders out of the temple with a whip. His triumphant entry and the cleansing of the temple made the religious leaders decide to get rid of Jesus (Matthew 21:15; Mark 11:18). They plotted against Him. Judas, one of the twelve disciples, betrayed Him and delivered Him into their hands. After having supper with His disciples, Jesus made His way to the garden of Gethsemane, a spot to which He often withdrew in order to pray. There, weighed down under the burden of human sin, Jesus experienced terrible anguish. In prayer,

He agreed of His own free will to offer His life as a sacrifice (Matthew 26:39). To the astonishment of the crowd, Jesus allowed Himself to be led away without resistance (John 18:3–12). He was taken to the High Priest, the religious leader, then to Pilate, the Roman governor, then brought before Herod, the king of the Jews. Jesus underwent the worst outrages, those which were normally reserved for the most wicked criminals. He was condemned without any valid accusation. When Pilate consulted the crowd they shouted, 'Crucify Him!'

The death of Jesus

Jesus was taken to Golgotha. He was nailed to a cross along with two criminals. When He was just about to die, and undergoing unspeakable sufferings, Jesus still spoke wonderful words. He prayed for His executioners, 'Father forgive them; for they do not know what they are doing' (Luke 23:34).

He put into practice what He Himself had taught: 'Love your enemies and pray for those who persecute you' (Matthew 5:44). In the sure knowledge that He had fulfilled in every detail the words of God revealed in the Old Testament, He cried out, 'It is finished!' (John 19:30).

He knew that He was offering the supreme sacrifice, which had been foretold by the prophets (Isaiah 53). Jesus died. The soldiers pierced His side, and blood and water flowed out. They took Him down from the cross. His body was placed in a new tomb and the tomb sealed with a large stone. His disciples were scattered. His work seemed to have come to nothing.

The death of Jesus is the central fact of the story of salvation. It is at the cross that the wall of sin was knocked down. That is why the cross remains the rallying cry of all Christians, who exclaim with the apostle Paul, 'But we preach Christ crucified' (1 Corinthians 1:23).

The resurrection of Jesus

According to Jewish custom the women prepared to

embalm the body of Jesus with perfume. But an un-expected event took place which transformed the disciples' despair into excitement and His enemies' victory into defeat—Jesus came out of the tomb on the morning of the first day of the week. That is why, ever since then, Christians have celebrated each Sunday as a day of resurrection (Acts 20:7). On that day, Jesus conquered death once and for all.

No, the disciples were not dreaming. The resurrection is a historical fact. First the women who went to embalm the body, and then Peter and John found the tomb empty. Jesus showed Himself alive, not to just one or two people, but to all His disciples. Even Thomas, who did not want to believe, was convinced when Jesus presented Himself before him (John 20:26–29). Paul tells us that Jesus 'appeared to more than five hundred brethren at one time' (1 Corinthians 15:6). The resurrection is therefore a definite fact.

The nature of the resurrection of Jesus

Unlike the raising to life of Lazarus (John 11), the resurrection of Jesus was not simply a return to this life. Certainly, the resurrected body was still the same body, as Thomas could see in it the marks made by the nails and by the sword (John 20:27). But after the resurrection this body was immortal (1 Corinthians 15:42–44). Death no longer had power over it. This new body was no longer bound by the laws of nature. In His spiritual, resurrection body, Jesus entered a room, while the doors and windows were closed (John 20:19). He had not become just a spirit, however. He Himself said to His frightened disciples: 'See My hands and My feet, that it is I Myself; touch Me and see, for a spirit does not have flesh and bones as you see that I have. ... He said to them, "Have you anything here to eat?" And they gave Him a piece of broiled fish; and He took it and ate it in their sight' (Luke 24:39,41–43).

The resurrection of Jesus is a promise

The apostle Paul in his letter to the Corinthians devotes a whole chapter to the resurrection (1 Corinthians 15). After refuting the arguments of those who cast doubt on the resurrection of Jesus, he states, 'But now Christ has been raised from the dead, the first fruits of those who are asleep' (1 Corinthians 15:20).

The resurrection of Jesus is a promise of our own resurrection. If He had remained in the tomb, how could we have known that God had accepted His sacrifice? But now we know that death has been conquered. We, too, shall receive an immortal body. The apostles received new strength from the resurrection of their Lord. Peter, who had denied Jesus, astonished the Jews. He spoke with authority. He was no longer the same man. We, too, can receive God's strength, if we believe that Jesus is really raised from the dead.

The ascension of Jesus

Forty days after the resurrection Jesus was taken up to heaven. Having finished His work on earth, He returned to the glory of heaven (Acts 1:9). His disciples had been forewarned: 'But I tell you the truth, it is to your advantage that I go away; for if I do not go away, the Helper shall not come to you; but if I go, I will send Him to you' (John 16:7).

Thus Jesus' departure leads on to Pentecost (Luke 24:49), the coming of the Holy Spirit in whom Jesus is 'with [us] always, even to the end of the age' (Matthew 28:20).

Christ's ascension also points forward to His coming again. No sooner had He gone, than angels appeared to the disciples and gave them a promise from God: 'This Jesus, who has been taken up from you into heaven, will come in just the same way as you have watched Him go into heaven' (Acts 1:11).

The work of Jesus Christ

The whole work which Jesus accomplished for our salvation can be summed up in a few biblical words. As these expressions are very rarely used in everyday speech, we have to explain them.

Redemption

This word comes from Latin, and means 'buying back'. In the apostles' day, redemption was the act of freeing a slave by paying his master the required price. In our day when slavery no longer exists, this expression no longer means much for us, but redemption was formerly a very clear picture of the work of Jesus. Indeed, ever since the Fall of Adam and Eve, men have been slaves of sin (Romans 6:6). But by giving His life, Christ has paid the price of their redemption: 'Knowing that you were not redeemed with perishable things like silver or gold from your futile way of life inherited from your forefathers, but with precious blood, as of a lamb unblemished and spotless, the blood of Christ' (1 Peter 1:18–19).

This sacrifice was offered to God (Hebrews 9:14), so that His justice should be satisfied. Since sin has been punished, God can receive us because the price of our freedom has been paid by Jesus Christ.

Atonement

The word is found mainly in the Old Testament. It means the act by which sin is covered by blood. Under the Old Covenant, that is, before the coming of Christ, it was the blood of lambs and oxen, and of all the animal sacrifices which served to make atonement for sin (Leviticus 17:11). But this blood of animals could not blot out sin. It pointed forward to the great sacrifice of Jesus. His blood, which represents His life offered up as a sacrifice, cleanses us from all sin (1 John 1:7).

African religions require a great number of sacrifices. But these sacrifices are hardly ever offered to the great

God, the Creator. They are rarely sacrifices to cover sin, rather they are offerings intended to attract the favour of a god or a spirit. Atonement is an idea which is found only in the Bible.

Justification

Justification is the consequence of redemption and atonement (Romans 4:25). When Jesus Christ has bought us back, and covered our sin by His blood, then we are fit to appear before God. Justification is therefore the act by which we are declared righteous. By this act, Jesus Christ has given us His righteousness as a gift, so that we can be saved.

Reconciliation

This word is sometimes used in everyday speech. When two men or two countries have had a quarrel and then they settle their dispute, we say they are reconciled. God has never been our enemy, but we have been the enemies of God because of our disobedience. Thanks to Christ's work of justification, communication can be re-established between the Creator and the creature (2 Corinthians 5:18).

Forgiveness

This is the act by which a fault is forgotten. Christ's work is perfect. It has blotted out all our sins and God has forgotten them for ever (Acts 13:38).

Grace

This word occurs very often in the Bible. It can have several different meanings. When it refers to the work of Christ it means an undeserved favour. Indeed, we have done nothing to deserve salvation. On the contrary, we have rebelled against God. It was right that we should be condemned. The apostle Paul declares, 'For by grace you

have been saved through faith; and that not of
yourselves, it is the gift of God' (Ephesians 2:8).

Sanctification

This is the work of Jesus Christ by which He sets us apart
for God (1 Corinthians 1:30). By justification, the
Christian becomes a citizen of the kingdom of God, but
he is still far from behaving like a disciple of Jesus Christ.
Only knowledge of the Word of God and the light of the
Holy Spirit can sanctify him, that is, make him lead the
new life of a citizen of the kingdom of God. Justification
gives us the right to enter the kingdom of God.
Sanctification is the change which salvation brings in the
life of the believer. Each Christian must seek 'the
sanctification without which no one will see the Lord'
(Hebrews 12:14).

Sanctification is the work of Jesus Christ living in us by
the Holy Spirit. In the third part of this book we shall see
what this means in practice.

4
The doctrine of the Holy Spirit

Who is the Holy Spirit?

The Holy Spirit is the Third Person of the Trinity of which we spoke in chapter 2. The word 'spirit' makes us think of all those mysterious beings to whom sacrifices are offered in the traditional African religions. But the Holy Spirit of God is not at all like any of these powers. He is *holy*, which means He is *separate*, entirely different from anything that man can imagine. The word 'spirit' means 'breath'. Breathing, or respiration, is a sign of life. The Holy Spirit is *God giving life* (Genesis 1:2).

The Holy Spirit is a Person

He is not simply an influence, a power similar to that of the wind which we cannot see, but which can be used if necessary. No, on the contrary, the Holy Spirit is a Master to whom we must listen. Several texts state that He is a Person. Paul declares that the Holy Spirit has a will of His own: 'But one and the same Spirit works all these things, distributing to each one individually just as He wills' (1 Corinthians 12:11).

Elsewhere, it is said that He can be grieved: 'And do not grieve the Holy Spirit of God ...' (Ephesians 4:30). Only a person can be grieved.

The Holy Spirit is God

He is not simply a servant of God like the angels, who are also spirits: 'Do you not know that you are a temple of God, and that the Spirit of God dwells in you?'

(1 Corinthians 3:16).

By the Holy Spirit, God the Father and Jesus Christ the Son are present in the heart of the believer (Romans 8:9; John 14:23; 1 John 3:24). If the Holy Spirit were not God, Paul could not say, 'You are a temple of God.'

The work of the Holy Spirit

The Bible tells us relatively little about the Person of the Holy Spirit, but it says a lot about His work. We shall sum up His main activities by a few verbs.

He *creates* (Job 33:4). This is how we see Him at work in the very beginning: 'In the beginning God created the heavens and the earth ... and the Spirit of God was moving over the surface of the waters' (Genesis 1:1–2).

He *convicts* men, that is, He causes them to recognize the truth of God and their own wretched state (John 16:8).

He *regenerates* (John 3). It is He, and He alone, who has the power to produce the miracle of the new birth.

He *seals* the believer, He puts on him a mark which certifies that he belongs to the people of God (2 Corinthians 1:22). It is He who gives assurance of salvation, the certainty that 'neither death, nor life ... nor any other created thing, shall be able to separate us from the love of God, which is in Christ Jesus our Lord' (Romans 8:38–39).

He *teaches* and brings to mind all that Jesus has said (John 14:26). Without His help, it is impossible for us to understand Scripture.

He *sanctifies* those whom He has regenerated, separating them from evil (1 Peter 1:2).

He *equips*, that is, He gives gifts, so that believers are able to become witnesses to Jesus Christ by His power (Acts 1:8).

The fruit and the gifts of the Holy Spirit

We must distinguish between the *fruit* of the Holy Spirit,

which all born-again believers must produce, and the *gifts* of the Holy Spirit, which are given 'to each one individually just as He wills' (1 Corinthians 12:11).

The fruit of the Holy Spirit is the result of the transformation which takes place in the life of those who no longer walk according to the flesh, but according to the Spirit (Galatians 5:13–25). The apostle Paul gives a detailed description of the fruit: 'But the fruit of the Spirit is love, joy, peace, patience, kindness, goodness, faithfulness, gentleness, self-control' (Galatians 5:22).

We must not forget that these fruits need to be cultivated by continual reading of and meditation on the Bible (Psalm 1:2–3).

The gifts of the Holy Spirit are given to the community of believers which Paul compares to a body in which all the members are at the same time very different and yet very closely bound together. Just as each member has a work to do for the good of the whole body, so each individual Christian receives a gift for the edification of the church (1 Corinthians 12:7). But for the exercise of these gifts to contribute truly to the building up of the church, several conditions must be fulfilled. Here are just three of them:

Firstly, no gift or experience can give rise to a doctrine or a teaching which would claim to add to the Bible. The Scriptures alone have authority.

Secondly, everything must be examined by the whole body in the light of Holy Scripture. It is on the subject of prophecy that Paul declares to the Thessalonians, 'Examine everything carefully; hold fast to that which is good' (1 Thessalonians 5:21). To say that something comes from the Holy Spirit when it does not, is to take the name of God in vain.

Thirdly, everything must be done in a proper and orderly way (1 Corinthians 14:40), for God 'is not a God of confusion but of peace' (1 Corinthians 14:33). Agitation and noise are not favourable to the exercise of spiritual gifts, but rather produce confusion.

The fulness of the Holy Spirit

This word 'fulness' is not found as such in the Bible, but it refers to a biblical truth which is often spoken of, either in exhortations, or in the accounts in the book of Acts. The evangelist Luke, in particular, tends to use the expression, 'to be filled with the Spirit'. The words of the Greek language in which he wrote, and the circumstances under which the apostles were filled with the Holy Spirit lead us to two conclusions. Firstly, there is a fulness which is manifest on *special occasions*. At Pentecost, and later when the apostles appeared before tribunals, and had to reply to those who accused them, the Holy Spirit revealed Himself suddenly, giving them exceptional power (Acts 2; Acts 4:8). Similarly, today the Holy Spirit fills those of His servants who find themselves in similar circumstances.

Also, when the apostle Paul exhorted the Ephesians saying, 'Be filled with the Spirit' (Ephesians 5:18), he was not referring only to the sudden and spectacular manifestation which the Holy Spirit permits in special circumstances, but to the constant presence of the Holy Spirit in the life of the believer. He lives in the believer's heart, in rather the way an important visitor lives in a friend's house (1 Corinthians 6:19). But if we have a guest in our house, we put a room at his disposal, but do not allow him to rummage everywhere. However, although the Holy Spirit is the guest of the Christian, He is in our hearts to put things in order, and therefore He must be able to go everywhere, and examine the most secret corners of our lives. To be filled with the Holy Spirit means to give Him the freedom to change everything in our lives that is not conformed to the Word of God.

This fulness shows itself in a life of love for God and for one's neighbour. When a Christian is filled with the Spirit in this way then, according to His all-powerful will, God may allow him to be filled with the Holy Spirit in a sudden and powerful fashion, if he is called to witness in particular circumstances. Finally, we should also say that it is possible to be filled with the Holy Spirit without knowing it. The important thing for the Christian is not to have spectacular experiences, but to be where God has placed him, usable, and in submission to the Word of God.

The sin against the Holy Spirit

Many Christians are troubled by these words of Jesus: 'Therefore I say to you, any sin and blasphemy shall be forgiven men, but blasphemy against the Spirit shall not be forgiven' (Matthew 12:31), and wonder if they might have committed that sin. Let those who ask themselves that question be reassured; if they had been guilty of blasphemy against the Spirit, they would no longer be worried about it. Indeed, if someone understands the Word of God, but does not repent, if he perseveres in his evil ways, he is despising the Holy Spirit (Hebrews 6:4–6). The day will come when the Holy Spirit will stop calling. The sin against the Holy Spirit consists in trampling underfoot the grace of God until it is withdrawn (Hebrews 10:26–27).

The existence of the unforgivable sin constitutes a warning for all those who do not take the message of the gospel seriously: 'Therefore, just as the Holy Spirit says, "Today if you hear His voice, do not harden your hearts ..." ' (Hebrews 3:7–8).

5
The doctrine of man

What is man?

This question has preoccupied thinkers all down the ages. But only God can give the true reply. Indeed, who is in a better position than He to reply? Since He is the Creator, He knows why He made man.

It is not possible to consider here all the questions concerning the creation of man, so we will concentrate on those which help us to know God and serve Him better.

The origin of man

The Bible is not a scientific treatise. But it reveals things which science would never be able to discover by its own methods. It declares, 'God created man in His own image, in the image of God He created him; male and female He created them' (Genesis 1:27).

Since God is our Creator, it is to Him that we shall have to give an account of the life He has given us (Ephesians 2:10). To believe in God as Creator, therefore, is to recognize that we owe Him obedience. That is why men who want to live for themselves persuade themselves that the world created itself! (Psalm 53:1).

Man is a responsible being

Scripture states that God created man 'in [His] own image, according to His likeness' (Genesis 1:26). It is perhaps in the gift of speech that the resemblance between God and man appears most clearly. That is what makes man into a *responsible* being, that is to say, *capable of responding*. Because of this ability, he can think, reflect and make decisions. Animals are guided by their instinct. But men are able to resist doing what their bodies urge them to do. Everything happens as if there were in man a being stronger than himself. This inner being, the Bible calls the 'heart'. From here come our thoughts and speech. It is our 'heart' which was created in the image of God.

The purpose of man's life

It was in love that God created man. He placed him in the garden of Eden where nothing was lacking ('Eden' means 'pleasure'). The only response to love is love. All that man did, was to be done out of love. He was meant to use intelligence and all his capabilities in the service of his Creator.

To act out of love and for the glory of God is the only way to be really happy. The purpose of man's life is the glory of God.

The Fall

There is no love without freedom. You cannot force someone to love! So God gave Adam and Eve a choice. He put before them their responsibility as free creatures: 'From the tree of the knowledge of good and evil you shall not eat, for in the day that you eat from it you shall surely die' (Genesis 2:17). The man and the woman were perfectly free to choose between God's knowledge and that which the forbidden tree could give them. In choosing what the tree had to offer, they thought they would no longer have need of God, they would become completely autonomous and independent (Genesis 3:5). Led astray by the words of the serpent, Adam and Eve chose independence. By disobeying, our first parents put up a wall of separation between God and men. This wall is called *sin*.

The results of the Fall

In rebelling against God, man lost sight of the purpose of his life. That is why the Bible states that man without God is dead (Ephesians 2:1). It is spiritual death. Man is like an electric light bulb. To light up, a lamp must be in contact with the electric current, a battery or a plug. If you take out the battery or pull out the plug, the lamp is still in working order, nothing has changed in the bulb, but it gives no light, just as if the bulb were useless. Similarly with man, if he is not in contact with God, his life has no meaning, he lives in darkness, fear and hatred: he has become a sinner. In order to find once more the purpose of his existence and forgiveness of sins, it is absolutely essential for him to re-establish contact with God. But he cannot do this by himself. Left to himself, man is incapable of doing good and being happy. King David, the psalmist, describes this miserable state: 'God has looked down from heaven upon the sons of men, to see if there is anyone who understands, who seeks after God. Every one of them has turned aside; together they have become corrupt; there is no one who does good, not even one' (Psalm 53:2–3).

Instead of serving God in freedom, man has become a slave to his evil desires. And as the child of a slave is also a slave, all mankind has been reduced to slavery (Psalm 51:5). The awful consequences of this are suffering and death.

Redemption

We have already seen that this word means 'buying back'. It is the act by which God saves us from the slavery of sin, thanks to the work of Jesus Christ. As soon as a man asks for God's grace, he is set free, he receives a new life. As the apostle Paul says, he is 'dead to sin' (Romans 6:11), that is to say, sin is no longer his master, although it remains in his body which has not yet been transformed, and Paul writes, 'Even we ourselves groan within ourselves, waiting eagerly for our adoption as sons, the redemption of our body' (Romans 8:23).

This complete change, which will finally deliver us from sin, suffering and death, will take place at the return of Jesus Christ (1 Corinthians 15:35–55).

Now, what happened when slaves were set free? As soon as someone paid the price of their redemption, they did not need to receive any more orders from their master. But they possessed nothing apart from their liberty, and they had to find somewhere to live. This is a little like what happens for the Christian. He is free, but he still lives in this world where Satan is the prince, until Christ comes for him.

All things really are new for him. He is truly free. But he is still living in the same world. He is no longer a slave, but he is surrounded by people who are slaves. He is therefore always in danger of going back to the old ways again! He must at all costs join with other freed slaves, and that is why Jesus Christ, the liberator, has founded the church, the community of all the redeemed. With the help of this new family where he is fed with the Word of God, and finds comfort in prayer and praise, the Christian learns to live as a citizen of the kingdom of God. We must therefore spend a chapter considering the church, so as to be able to understand how it is different from all other human societies.

6

The doctrine of the church

The church is the people of God

Under the Old Covenant, before the coming of Jesus Christ, the people of God consisted of all the descendants of Abraham. It was a people related to each other by birth. But the church is a spiritual people. All those who are set free from the slavery of sin are part of it. They are one, not because of their common ancestors, but because the Holy Spirit of God has put new life in them. The church therefore is not a human society like others, but is primarily the people of God.

Definition

The word 'church' comes from a Greek word which means 'called out of'. The church is all those whom God has called out of the world to save them. But the word 'church' in the New Testament refers to two distinct aspects of the people of God. That is why we distinguish between the church and local churches.

The church: When the apostle Paul declares, 'Christ ... loved the church' (Ephesians 5:25), he is referring to the whole body of those whom Jesus Christ has redeemed. This church has been described as 'invisible' because one can neither see nor count who belongs to it. Only God knows those who belong to it (2 Timothy 2:19). This church has also been called 'universal' because it is made up of *all* Christians of *all* times and in *all* places.

The local churches: When Paul wrote to the Corinthians and sent his greetings in the following words: 'Paul ...

and Sosthenes our brother, to the church of God which is at Corinth ...' (1 Corinthians 1:1–2), he was referring to a local and visible community. Anyone could know who belonged to this church. Anywhere that a number of Christians meet together in the name of Jesus Christ, practising baptism and observing the Lord's Supper, there is a local church. We have been given several pictures to help us understand how Christians are united among themselves in the church, and how the church is united to Jesus Christ.

The church as the body of Christ

Christ has authority over the church which is His body (1 Corinthians 12:27; Ephesians 5:23).

This illustration explains several important points. The human body is very complex, with many members all of which are very different from each other (1 Corinthians 12:14–15). Each has a function to be useful to the whole body.

The picture of the body emphasizes first of all the *diversity* of the members of the body. In the church there are young and old, illiterate and educated, rich and poor, black and white. In the churches there are pastors, evangelists, deacons, singers and ordinary Christians who bear witness at their work and among their neighbours. The churches themselves may have different names, and worship in different ways. But the important thing is that each member of the church and each individual local church must be in submission to Jesus Christ the Head of the church, the Head of the body.

Then, the picture of the body also emphasizes the *unity* of the church. Paul declares, 'But now there are many members, but one body' (1 Corinthians 12:20).

The church of Jesus Christ, the universal church is one. All those who truly belong to Jesus Christ are united in Him, even if human differences of race, language and denomination remain. But this unity which exists between all true children of God, *must be shown*. All too often Christians or churches despise other Christians or other churches. It also happens too often that more importance is attached to race, or to church leaders than to the one thing necessary—Jesus Christ and His Word. The apostle Paul reproaches the Corinthians for their divisions: 'Now I exhort you, brethren, by the name of our Lord Jesus Christ, that you all agree, and there be no divisions among you, but you be made complete in the same mind and in the same judgement' (1 Corinthians 1:10).

The unity of churches can only come about by obedience to the Word of Jesus Christ and by concern to see brotherly love reigning. We cannot be in agreement on every point, but let us hold fast to Jesus Christ as the one and only Saviour and let us work together, asking God to give us more light (Philippians 3:15–16).

The church as the bride of Christ

The church is several times called the bride of Christ (Revelation 21:2,9). This illustration emphasizes the love which unites Jesus Christ to His church. This love is such that Jesus Christ 'gave Himself up for her' (Ephesians 5:25).

As Jesus Christ gave Himself for His church, so the church's one concern should be to give itself heart and soul to its Lord and Saviour. As an engaged girl lives for her wedding, and gets ready for it with joy, so the church should prepare itself for the great day of the return of Christ: ' "Let us rejoice and be glad and give the glory to Him, for the marriage of the Lamb has come and His bride has made herself ready." And it was given to her to clothe herself in fine linen, bright and clean; for the fine linen is the righteous acts of the saints' (Revelation 19:7–8).

As the righteous acts of Christians are like a wedding garment, the life and conduct of the Christian should be upright and should show forth his love for Christ his Saviour (1 Corinthians 13).

The mission of the church

Just before He went up into heaven, Jesus gave instructions to His disciples and through them to the whole church: 'You shall receive power when the Holy Spirit has come upon you; and you shall be My witnesses both in Jerusalem, and in all Judea and Samaria, and even to the remotest part of the earth' (Acts 1:8).

The church does not exist for itself; it has been given a task, a mission. A church which does not evangelize is disobeying its Lord and consequently cannot be blessed. This mission has not been entrusted only to pastors and evangelists, but to the whole church, to each individual Christian.

How much time do I give to bringing the good news to those who do not know it? Do my neighbours and the members of my family who are not yet Christians have a significant place in my prayers? What proportion of my possessions do I dedicate for evangelism? These are questions which we must all ask ourselves. Finally, let us remember that it is primarily by our daily actions and our attitude in little things, in a word, by our love for our fellow men, that our witness will bring forth fruit. 'Keep your behaviour excellent among the Gentiles, so that in the thing in which they slander you as evildoers, they may on account of your good deeds, as they observe them, glorify God in the day of visitation' (1 Peter 2:12).

7

The doctrine of baptism and the Lord's Supper

Why baptism and the Lord's Supper?

These acts have been commanded by Jesus Christ Himself to help us to understand better what He has done for us. These two ceremonies are not some kind of magical rites which are supposed to confer salvation or some privilege on those who receive them. But, like the Word, they proclaim the good news of salvation. Baptism and the Lord's Supper tell the message visually by actions, instead of by words.

The person who is baptized is acting out a role. He confesses by his actions that the death and resurrection of Jesus Christ blot out his sin, just as water washes his body.

Similarly, when he partakes of the Lord's Supper, he is proclaiming the grace of Christ. As he feeds on the bread and wine and receives strength from them, so he is stating that only the grace of Jesus Christ gives him life.

Baptism is a sign of identity

Under the Old Covenant, one became a member of the people of God by *birth*. Circumcision was a mark of identity which proved that a man belonged to the people of Israel. It was carried out in the flesh, because the nation was made up of all the descendants of one man, Abraham. But nowadays, one enters the people of God by the *new birth*. This new people, the universal church, is a spiritual people. It is no longer a physical, visible mark which proves that someone belongs to this people, but a spiritual, invisible mark—the baptism of the Holy Spirit

(Romans 2:29; 2 Corinthians 1:22). A person who is saved has the assurance that he belongs to God's people because 'the Spirit Himself bears witness with our spirit that we are children of God' (Romans 8:16).

But this internal mark is not enough. We need an external, visible mark. We live in a world where we are foreigners and pilgrims (1 Peter 2:11). We must have a mark of identity which shows that we are citizens of the kingdom of God. This mark of identity is water baptism. It is not the baptism itself which makes us citizens of the kingdom of God. One can easily be a true citizen of a country without possessing an identity card. But although baptism does not actually save us, it shows openly that we are members of God's people.

Baptism and the work of Jesus Christ

Every identity card states the place of birth of the holder. Similarly, baptism indicates where and how we were born into God's kingdom: 'Or do you not know that all of us who have been baptized into Christ Jesus have been baptized into His death? Therefore we have been buried with Him through baptism into death, in order that as Christ was raised from the dead through the glory of the Father, so we too might walk in newness of life' (Romans 6:3–4).

It is death and resurrection which have made the new birth possible. That is why baptism is a picture of the death and resurrection of the Lord.

As one enters the universal church by the baptism of the Holy Spirit, so one enters the local church by water baptism. The local church is an embassy of God's people in the world. It confers this sign of identity on all those who confess by their words and their actions that Jesus Christ has caused them to be born again into a new life.

The Lord's Supper and the Passover

In memory of their coming out of Egypt, God had ordained a feast which the Israelites were to celebrate each year (Exodus 12). The disciples of Jesus observe their feast, no longer to commemorate the deliverance from Egypt, but the deliverance from the curse of sin. The Passover recalled the release from slavery and foretold the sacrifice of the Messiah. The Lord's Supper recalls the sacrifice of Jesus—'Do this in remembrance of me' (1 Corinthians 11:24) and foretells His return in glory: 'For as often as you eat this bread and drink the cup, you proclaim the Lord's death until He comes' (1 Corinthians 11:26).

The Lord's Supper and fellowship

Sometimes the Lord's Supper is called 'communion'. This reminds us that this supper demonstrates the brotherly love which unites the disciples of Jesus Christ. Indeed 'dipping one's hand in the dish together' is the action which best expresses brotherly love. But the bread which represents the body of Jesus and the wine, the symbol of His blood, show at what tremendous cost this fellowship has been established.

How we should take the Lord's Supper

The solemn nature of this meal demands that one should not take it lightly. Because they had profaned it, several Christians in the Corinthian church had become ill, and some had even died (1 Corinthians 11:30). That is why the apostle Paul writes to the Corinthians, 'But let a man examine himself, and so let him eat of the bread and drink of the cup. For he who eats and drinks, eats and drinks judgement to himself, if he does not judge the body rightly' (1 Corinthians 11:28).

Who can take part in this meal then? It is not a

question of being perfect, for then no one could partake of it. But we must approach the Lord's table with a repentant heart and with faith.

Jesus gave us these visible signs, baptism and the Lord's Supper, to help us in our faith. They are not indispensable to salvation, but Christians cannot neglect them without running the risk of growing cold in their spiritual lives.

8

The doctrine of the last things

What is there beyond death?

The Bible teaches that death is not the end of everything. It tells us of a world to come which it calls eternity. But it describes it in picture language, because we are completely unable to imagine the visible world after death. How can human words describe something that is beyond human imagination? We are so attached to this earth that we are like caterpillars crawling on the ground. Can a caterpillar imagine that one day it will become a butterfly with gorgeous wings? It cannot even understand the meaning of the words 'to fly'. That is why we should not try to imagine what eternity will be like. We must be content with what the Bible tells us.

After death

All who have placed their trust in Jesus Christ go into His presence when they die (2 Corinthians 5:8). Indeed, just as He was about to die on the cross, Jesus said to the repentant robber, 'Truly I say to you, today you shall be with Me in Paradise' (Luke 23:43).

Those who have not made their peace with God have to wait in the terrifying expectation of the judgement to come (Hebrews 10:27; John 5:29). Contrary to traditional African beliefs, the souls of the dead do not remain on earth. Therefore the dead can never intervene in the lives of the living.

The return of Jesus Christ

At a moment which only God knows (Matthew 24:36),

Jesus will come again in person for His people: 'For the Lord Himself will descend from heaven with a shout, with the voice of the archangel, and with the trumpet of God; and the dead in Christ shall rise first. Then we who are alive and remain shall be caught up together with them in the clouds to meet the Lord in the air, and thus we shall always be with the Lord' (1 Thessalonians 4:16–17).

At the moment of Christ's return, the miracle of the resurrection will take place. The dead in Christ will rise, the believers who are still alive will be changed, and we shall all go together to our heavenly homeland.

The judgement

For those who have despised the Word of God, the return of Christ will be terrifying: 'And then the sign of the Son of Man will appear in the sky, and then all the tribes of the earth will mourn, and they will see the Son of Man coming on the clouds of the sky with power and great glory' (Matthew 24:30).

It is then that the judgement will take place. Each one will be judged according to his works (Matthew 25:31–46; Revelation 20:12). God will be perfectly just (Romans 2:12,16). Jesus says on this subject, 'And that slave who knew his master's will and did not get ready or act in accord with his will, shall receive many lashes, but the one who did not know it, and committed deeds worthy of a flogging, will receive but few' (Luke 12:47–48).

The condemnation

Let us not take the place of God—neither in deciding for ourselves who will be judged, nor in describing the suffering of those who are condemned (Revelation 20:10). What we do know with certainty, because the Bible clearly states it, is, 'The Lord Jesus shall be revealed from heaven with His mighty angels in flaming fire, dealing out retribution to those who do not know God and to those who do not obey the gospel of our Lord Jesus. And these will pay the penalty of eternal destruction, away from the presence of the Lord and from the glory of His power' (2 Thessalonians 1:7–9). We must therefore be very zealous to bring the good news of salvation to those who do not know God.

Eternal salvation

The redeemed will come before the judgement seat of Christ (2 Corinthians 5:10). There the Lord will deal with each one according to the faithfulness he has shown during his life on earth (1 Corinthians 3:13–15). Then they will be always in the presence of God. They will enjoy perfect happiness such as is impossible to imagine.

9

The doctrine of angels

Who are the angels?

The word comes from the Greek language. It means 'messenger'. They are all 'ministering spirits, sent out to render service for the sake of those who will inherit salvation' (Hebrews 1:14).

They are depicted in paintings as having wings. But there is no evidence that they have any particular distinctive appearance, for it is written, 'Do not neglect to show hospitality to strangers, for by this some have entertained angels without knowing it' (Hebrews 13:2).

There seems to be a hierarchy among the angels, that is, they have leaders, the archangels (Jude 9).

What do angels do?

They intervene on God's behalf. It was the angel Gabriel who announced to Mary that she was going to give birth to the Saviour (Luke 1:26). It was an angel who delivered Peter from prison (Acts 12:7). God also sends angels to carry out His judgements (Acts 12:23).

But there is one question which is particularly important for us: do the angels intervene in our lives? The Bible states, 'The angel of the Lord encamps around those who fear Him, and rescues them' (Psalm 34:7).

Daniel's friends were protected in the furnace by an angel (Daniel 3:28). God's angels watch over children (Matthew 18:10). So God can send them to help us if that is His will (Psalm 91:11). But even though this is true, we must not put our trust in them. We must neither worship them, nor pray to them (Colossians 2:18).

Satan

This word means 'adversary', 'enemy'. He is the enemy
of God. In the beginning he is thought to have been an
archangel in the armies of the Lord. But, in a revolt,
about which we know only very little, he became the
great enemy of God. He is also called the devil. This word,
in the Bible, has nothing to do with the belief that some
men change into animals. The word 'devil' comes from
the Greek. In this language it means 'the one who
divides'. That is how Satan works. Wherever he goes, he
sows division, hatred, wickedness, that is to say, all that is
the opposite of love.

Satan is also called the ruler of this world (John 12:31).
His power is very great. But he cannot do anything that
he wants. When he attacked Job, he could do nothing
without God's permission (Job 2:6). He is like a lion on a
chain, with God holding the chain.

Demons and evil spirits

These mysterious beings do exist; Jesus believed in them.
During His ministry He cast out a number of them. In
doing this, Jesus taught us not to be afraid of them. But
we must be very careful to get rid of anything that could
have been used by them. Fetishes, especially, must be
destroyed. Many Christians lead a miserable existence.
They fall back into all sorts of sins; they no longer have
the joy of their salvation. Why is this? It is because they
have not completely broken with the power of Satan.
Perhaps they have not confessed to God that they once
consulted a medium. Perhaps they have a mysterious
name given them by a charlatan. Everything, absolutely
everything must be confessed to God. We should not fear
Satan and the evil spirits, because Jesus has conquered
them. But we should be convinced that they are capable
of doing a lot of harm. Satan is very cunning. To be even
more effective, he does everything he can so that people
do not believe in his power. This is a very intelligent

tactic, similar to that of soldiers who hide among the trees so that no one believes they are there. The Christian who is aware of the danger puts into practice Paul's advice: 'Put on the full armour of God, that you may be able to stand firm against the schemes of the devil' (Ephesians 6:11).

Contrary to popular belief, the Bible states that Satan and the demons will be those who will suffer the most in eternity: 'Depart from Me, accursed ones, into the eternal fire which has been prepared for the devil and his angels' (Matthew 25:41).

Part 2 How to become a Christian

Man can do nothing to save himself

Our actions have no merit

The traditional African religions teach that God will judge men. He will weigh their actions. Those who have done good during their life on earth will inherit happiness. Those who have done evil will be punished. The Bible, too, states that God will judge men according to their works. But it declares that all men are lost, because all, without exception, do evil: 'There is none who does good, there is not even one' (Romans 3:12).

Under these conditions, no one can be saved. Even those who make great efforts to do good cannot win God's favour. Why is it that God cannot take into account the good done by lost men? It is because God is holy (see chapter 2). All that man can do remains infected by sin (Isaiah 64:5). The story is told of a king who was invited to a conciliatory meal. His subjects, who wanted to be forgiven by their king, had organized a great feast for him. They had prepared a great number of dishes. The meal had cost them a lot of money. But the king could not touch any of it. Why? The delicious food was served using dirty plates and dishes! The works of men are like this. While the human heart remains infected with sin, God cannot accept what we offer Him.

There is no salvation except in Jesus Christ

We often hear it said that all religions are good as long as a person is sincere. This is not the opinion of the Bible. Since our works are worth nothing, all religions are equally incapable of bringing salvation. A man who has fallen to the bottom of a pit is completely incapable of getting out by himself. He needs to have a rope flung to him by someone at the top. Only God could throw us this rope, and He has done it. In His Word, He declares about Jesus Christ, 'There is salvation in no one else; for there is no other name under heaven that has been given among men, by which we must be saved' (Acts 4:12).

Jesus Himself said when He was on earth, 'I am the way, and the truth, and the life; no one comes to the Father, but through Me' (John 14:6).

The story is told of a village where all the inhabitants were ill. The water from their well smelt bad. This was the source of their illness. The village chief gave orders that the well should be cleaned. But the water remained bad. He had large quantities of sugar thrown into it. That did not make any difference. In desperation, they offered sacrifices to their ancestors, but without any result. Finally, someone offered to go down to the bottom of the well. There he discovered a sheep's carcass. Once the well was completely emptied, and cleared of this refuse, it gave pure water.

This story explains in a simple way why only Jesus Christ can save us. He alone is able to cleanse our hearts from sin. But this salvation is not given to men automatically, without any response on their part to the grace which God offers them.

The act by which lost man takes hold of this salvation is described in the Bible by several different words. We tend, all too easily, to think that all these expressions mean exactly the same thing. All of them do indeed speak to us about the way we receive salvation, but each of these words describes a different aspect of the question. In the following chapters we shall explain these words in some detail.

11

Faith

Faith is absolutely essential for salvation (Hebrews 11:6)

The word 'faith' occurs often in the Bible. The Old Testament does not use the actual word as often as the New Testament, but it includes many stories of men and women who had faith. The whole Bible insists on the fact that it is by faith that one becomes a Christian: 'For by grace you have been saved through faith; and that not of yourselves, it is the gift of God' (Ephesians 2:8).

The Christian must also live by faith: 'The righteous will live by his faith' (Habakkuk 2:4).

Definition

It is difficult to define this word adequately in a few lines. There are three elements in faith: belief, trust and obedience.

1. Belief

To believe means to be sure that something is true. When it was announced on radio and television that man had set foot on the moon, we had to believe something. Was it true or not? Some people did not believe it.

When Paul and Silas replied to the Philippian jailer, 'Believe in the Lord Jesus, and you shall be saved' (Acts 16:31), they meant: believe in your heart that Jesus really died and is risen again. Be sure that He is really able to save you. Many people think that belief is contrary to reason. These people do not want to believe in God because they have never seen Him. However, faith is not opposed to sight, but concerning the invisible things of the kingdom of God we walk by faith (2 Corinthians 5:7). Thus we can say that faith is seeing with the heart. But all men's hearts are blind unless God heals them (1 Corinthians 2:9–10). That is why it is written, 'By grace you have been saved through faith; and that not of yourselves, it is the gift of God' (Ephesians 2:8).

2. Trust

It is not enough to believe that a surgeon is capable of removing whatever is causing your illness. You have to go further and put your confidence in him by actually going to the operating table. There are many people who believe that Jesus Christ really existed. They do not doubt His death and resurrection, but that makes no difference to their lives. Mere belief in Jesus is not enough, we must also allow Him to transform our lives. To explain what it means to trust, Jesus took a child, and placed him in the midst of His disciples saying, 'Unless you ... become like children, you shall not enter the kingdom of heaven' (Matthew 18:3).

Trustful faith is precisely the attitude which a child has towards his parents. He is aware of his weakness and he believes that his parents can do everything. He trusts in them for everything. The story is told of a little boy who was helping his father cut away the undergrowth in the family plantation. Suddenly, a panther appeared out of the forest. What did the child do? He had a machete in his hand, so he was able to defend himself. But no, he did not defend himself, he ran to take refuge beside his father. That was much more sensible. That is what trustful faith is. As we face God's condemnation for our sin, or as we struggle with temptation, let us not struggle by our own efforts, but let us call on God's help.

3. Obedience

When God has delivered us, we should be filled with thankfulness towards Him. This thankfulness must be expressed, not only in words, but also in actions. That is why the apostle James writes, 'For just as the body without the spirit is dead, so also faith without works is dead' (James 2:26).

Obedience is therefore *a proof* of our faith in God. A man's actions have no merit; they are totally incapable of saving him. But when a man is saved by faith in Jesus Christ, he gives up his old way of life to walk in the path of obedience to God. Actions are not the beginning of faith, but the result of it.

12

Conversion and repentance

What is conversion?

When preaching the gospel, the apostles said, 'Repent therefore and return, that your sins may be wiped away, in order that times of refreshing may come from the presence of the Lord' (Acts 3:19).

Definition

Conversion is the act by which a person turns from the way in which the men of the world walk, to walk in God's way. It is not an effort to improve but the complete change which takes place when Jesus Christ transforms a whole life.

When a girl becomes engaged, a sort of conversion takes place. She stops living for her parents. She no longer thinks of herself, she lives only for her future husband. All her decisions are governed by her love for her fiancé. She devotes all her time to him.

This is exactly what must happen in the life of anyone who receives Jesus Christ as Lord and Saviour. He ceases to live for himself and for the world. From that time onwards he lives for God and for his fellow men. Wordly people seek their own glory. They are looking for success. They are attached to material things. The disciple of Jesus Christ has left all that behind. His one aim is to give glory to God.

False conversions

Unfortunately, these do exist. Those who have a desire to be saved, but who still keep in their lives masters other than Jesus Christ, are not truly converted. Some do not leave their love of money, others secretly hold on to fetishes. Soon their faith in Jesus Christ will be stifled (Matthew 13:1–23).

The book of Acts tells us the story of Simon the sorcerer (Acts 8:9–24). He had believed. He had even been baptized. But he had become converted because he hoped to gain something: he wanted to possess the power of the apostles for his own glory. It was a false conversion. We do not have the right to judge our brothers in the faith by saying, 'So-and-so is not converted.' But we must watch over ourselves (1 Corinthians 10:12). Let us serve no other masters besides Jesus Christ.

What is repentance?

The meaning of this expression is very close to that of the word 'conversion'. Repentance is part of conversion. But while a person is converted only once in his life, he has, alas, to keep on repenting.

Definition

The verb 'to repent' in the language of the writers of the New Testament means 'to change one's way of thinking'. Repentance is the act by which I leave my human way of thinking for God's thinking. Men do not take sin very seriously. For them, lying, pride or impurity are not very serious things. By repentance, a man recognizes that he is wrong. He recognizes that his heart and his thoughts are evil and that sin is a very serious matter.

If men were willing to acknowledge when they were in the wrong there would be no more wars! But no one is willing to admit that he can be mistaken. Everyone wants to be in the right. That is why peace is not possible. To repent is to acknowledge that God alone is right.

The signs of repentance

There is first of all sadness at having offended God, at having caused Him pain. Sincere repentance can sometimes lead to tears. In Psalm 51, King David, who had committed a very serious sin, has left us a prayer of repentance which is most instructive. It teaches us that another sign of sincere repentance is a deep desire to be delivered for ever from one's sin. Finally, true repentance must not be merely a matter of feelings, but it must produce fruit. John the Baptist said to those who came to be baptized with the baptism of repentance: 'Therefore bring forth fruit in keeping with your repentance' (Matthew 3:8).

Zaccheus, the tax collector, has left us a good example of the fruits of repentance. He said to Jesus, 'If I have defrauded anyone of anything, I will give back four times as much' (Luke 19:8).

God does not always ask us to give back four times as much, but He wants to see us putting right our faults when that is possible.

13
The new birth

What is the new birth?

Jesus said to Nicodemus, 'Truly, truly, I say to you, unless one is born again, he cannot see the kingdom of God' (John 3:3). Shocked by this statement, Nicodemus, the theologian, asked, 'How can a man be born when he is old?' (John 3:4).

Jesus explained to him that man is evil: what is born of flesh is flesh (John 3:6). Before we can be saved and see the kingdom of God, it is necessary for God Himself to put new life in us—eternal life.

Definition

The new birth is the act by which the Holy Spirit of God puts a new life in the heart of the believer. As a result, it is possible to become a child of God (John 1:12). The new birth shows clearly that salvation is the work of the Holy Spirit.

Conversion underlines the outward change, which appears in everyday life. The new birth shows clearly that this change comes from within, from a transformation of the heart by the Holy Spirit.

In talking about the new birth the apostle Paul also uses the word 'regeneration' (Titus 3:5). This expression means exactly same thing.

Assurance of salvation

There are some Christians who remember the exact date of their new birth. They can recount the exact cir-

cumstances in which it took place. This does not mean
that it is essential to know the date of one's new birth!
What is important is to be sure of having received a new
life (1 John 5:13). For some people it was a sudden
experience. Overnight their existence was completely
changed. For others, and perhaps for the children of
believers in particular, it is much more difficult to speak
of a spectacular change. What we should be able to state
without hesitation, is that we belong to Jesus Christ and
that we are 'convinced that neither death, nor life, nor
angels, nor principalities, nor things present, nor things
to come, nor powers, nor height, nor depth, nor any
other created thing, shall be able to separate us from the
love of God, which is in Christ Jesus our Lord' (Romans
8:38-39).

This assurance of being saved, the absolute conviction
that '*nothing* can separate us from the love of God', is not
a certainty based on personal feelings. The Bible states it
very clearly (Hebrews 7:25). Jesus Himself said, 'I give
eternal life to them [My sheep], and they shall never
perish; and no one shall snatch them out of My hand'
(John 10:28).

Assurance of salvation is therefore not based on the
hope that *we* shall remain in the right path, but on the
certainty that *God* will keep us there.

The old man and the new man

The new birth is a new beginning. From now on the
presence of the Holy Spirit in the believer's heart enables
him to conquer sin. The regenerate man can cry with the
apostle Paul, 'If any man is in Christ, he is a new
creature; the old things passed away; behold, new things
have come' (2 Corinthians 5:17).

However, we must not imagine that the born-again
believer will have no more difficulties. The Holy Spirit
gives him strength to conquer. But to speak of
conquering, implies a battle. The Christian must indeed
fight a very fierce battle. He is born again, but his old

sinful nature has not disappeared. A Christian's heart is like a piece of ground which has just been prepared for sowing. The field is clear, all the thorns and undergrowth have been destroyed. But after only a few days the weeds grow again. Sin is like this. Its root remains in us. We need to keep a careful watch over our hearts. Otherwise we run the risk of being overrun again by sin (Hebrews 12:1). The apostle Paul calls this part of us, which urges us to sin, 'the flesh' (Romans 8:12–13). He also calls it 'the old man'. Our flesh, or our old man, has been crucified (Colossians 3:9; Romans 6:6; Galatians 5:24). But as long as we live in the body, we shall have to struggle against our evil desires. One Christian thought that he had finally conquered his sin. But after some time he had to recognize that he could not call a truce. He described how he had been mistaken, saying, 'I was satisfied that I had drowned my old man, but then I realized that he could swim!'

How can we overcome?

Consequently, everything happens as if there were two men inside us: the old man, who no longer has any authority, but who never ceases to influence us towards evil, and the new man who is in control, but whose authority we must recognize. How can we know which of the two is speaking when a desire is born in our hearts? We must use the Word of God to decide. All desires which are not in accordance with the Word, come from the flesh. When we carry out what the Scriptures command us, we are always acting in the interests of the new man. That is why a knowledge of the Bible is so important. Finally, victory is only possible by the strength of the Holy Spirit: 'For it is God who is at work in you, both to will and to work for His good pleasure' (Philippians 2:13).

We must not imagine that we are able to conquer in our own strength.

Part 3 What the Christian life means in practice

14
What is the Christian life?

The true meaning of life re-discovered

Since the Fall, God's image in the heart of man has been defaced. Instead of using his intelligence and speech for good, man puts them to the service of evil. Instead of being like God, he resembles Satan, the father of lies. God had said, 'Let Us make man in Our image, according to Our likeness' (Genesis 1:26).

Why did God make man in His image? Because God wanted man to be His son, and because nothing gives a father more pleasure than to have a child who takes after him. But by disobeying the Creator, man began to resemble Satan! What would a father say if his son began to take after his worst enemy? Would not this be more painful than even the death of his son? God could no longer bear the sight of the man whom He had created. He had to break off relations with man. But as we have already seen, God did not cease to love men. He did the impossible to save them. Jesus Christ has made them a gift of His perfect righteousness, and the Holy Spirit gives them a new life. From now on, those who receive this salvation rediscover the true meaning of life. They can again resemble God and become His sons (1 John 3:1–2; John 1:12).

The duty of a son

Traditional religions require sacrifices, sometimes even great sacrifices which must be carried out in fear and trembling. But this is not how God wants us to serve Him (Romans 8:15). The Christian life is not made up of customs which we observe without understanding them.

There are no mysterious taboos to respect. God does not want the Christian to serve Him like a slave. He is a Father. He loves us. Even if we do not always understand His plans, we have the assurance that what He does is for our good. The duty of a Christian is the duty of a son towards his father. A son knows that one day, everything will belong to him (Romans 8:17). Until that day comes, he is submissive to his father in everything. Because he loves his father this obedience is not a painful duty. African customs give a very important place to respect for the father. Until his death, the father's advice is listened to about everything. He takes care of the whole house, and everyone surrounds him with great respect. Traditional family life is a lovely picture of what the Christian life should be. God takes care of us in every detail and in return we owe Him our obedience. There are two ways of understanding the Law of God. The first way considers it as the law of a hard and severe Master. The Law of God becomes demanding and the Christian life is sad. The second way sees in God's commandments the recommendations of a very loving Father. Then the Christian life becomes sweet and joyful (Psalm 119:97; 1 John 5:3).

The aim of the Christian life

The Christian should be like his heavenly Father. A son must get to know all that his father does. In the traditional way of life, the son of a blacksmith would become a blacksmith, too. From earliest childhood, the son watches his father. Little by little, he carries out simple tasks of his own. As he grows up, he learns the secrets of the trade. Eventually he becomes capable of doing everything that his father does. This is how things should be for the Christian. As he lives in the presence of God, he will learn to behave like his heavenly Father. Jesus said, 'Therefore you are to be perfect, as your heavenly Father is perfect' (Matthew 5:48). It is also written in the Old Testament: 'Be holy; for I am holy' (Leviticus 11:44).

Since God speaks to us in His Word, the Bible, the first duty of a Christian is to get to know this Word. It tells us what God has done. It also tells us who He is. It invites us to imitate Him in everything, to love Him as He has loved us. In Jesus Christ, God has given us a perfect example. We should not compare ourselves with other people, but with Him alone (Philippians 2:5). This is the only way of making true progress in the Christian life. That is why we must know God to be able to serve Him better.

In the following chapters we shall examine what God says in His Word about the life of the Christian. First of all we shall see the attitude of the Christian towards his God, then towards his fellow men and material things. Then we shall study the biblical teaching on the Christian and community life, the Christian and the world, the Christian and the state, and, finally, the Christian and the local church.

15

The Christian before God

The Christian and prayer

Living out the Christian life means, for all those who
engage in it whole-heartedly, numerous difficulties,
temptations, failures and sometimes discouragements.
To be like our heavenly Father in fulfilling the
requirements of His Law, involves fierce conflict. It is
only by drawing strength from God Himself that we can
come out victorious. This powerful God is not remote,
but by the Holy Spirit, He fulfils the promise of Jesus: 'I
am with you always, even to the end of the age' (Matthew
28:20). Only the assurance of God's presence can give us
the strength to lead a life which glorifies Him. But God is
pleased when we call to Him for help. He wants His
children to come and ask Him for what they need. So, in
the secrecy of his heart, the child of God prays to his
heavenly Father all the time (Matthew 6:6).

Prayer is like breathing—you cannot live long without
breathing! Anyone who stops praying gradually grows
colder and colder. Prayer is therefore a vital necessity for
the Christian. The apostle Paul said, 'Pray without
ceasing' (1 Thessalonians 5:17).

At any moment, in the secrecy of his heart, the
Christian can speak to his God. But it is also necessary to
reserve a special time each day for prayer, preferably in a
quiet place. 'When you pray, go into your inner room,
and when you have shut your door, pray to your Father
who is in secret' (Matthew 6:6).

A conversation between a son and a father implies that
there is a response from the father. In prayer we speak to
God, but how does He reply to us? By His Word the
Bible. That is why prayer is inseparable from reading of,
and meditation on Holy Scripture.

But there is a risk that we may pray in the wrong way, and may even introduce pagan customs into our prayers. Jesus warned His disciples of this danger: 'And when you are praying, do not use meaningless repetition, as the Gentiles do, for they suppose that they will be heard for their many words. Therefore do not be like them; for your Father knows what you need, before you ask Him' (Matthew 6:7–8).

Therefore it is of first importance to know how to pray and that is why Jesus has given His disciples a model prayer. It is not a question of merely repeating it word for word, but of understanding it so well that all our prayers follow this pattern.

The Lord's prayer

'Our Father who art in heaven,
Hallowed be Thy name.
Thy kingdom come.
Thy will be done,
On earth as it is in heaven.
Give us this day our daily bread.
And forgive us our debts, as we also have forgiven our
    debtors.
And do not lead us into temptation, but deliver us
    from evil.
For Thine is the kingdom, and the power, and the
    glory, forever. Amen' (Matthew 6:9–13).

'Our Father who art in heaven'

In inviting us to address God in this way, Jesus teaches us two truths. First of all, God is our Father and when we approach Him we should pray to Him with complete confidence. As He is our Father, He knows what we need better than we do. Secondly, this Father is not just any father: He is in heaven; He is the Creator and sovereign Master of the universe. We may approach Him freely since He is our Father. But when we come before Him it must be with great humility. Without Jesus Christ it would be impossible for us to speak to Him.

The rest of this prayer is divided into six requests. The first three concern the glory of God and the other three concern our own needs. In giving priority to the glory of God, Jesus teaches us to give second place to our own needs.

'Hallowed be Thy name'

That means, 'May the holiness of Your name be acknowledged.' To hallow the name of God means to place it above all other names. A name represents the person himself along with all that he does. In this prayer, the follower of Christ recognizes that, in his life and in the whole world, only the name of God is worthy of being worshipped. He asks that God should be acknowledged and worshipped as Creator and the only Lord, who does all things perfectly.

'Thy kingdom come'

God is the King, the Master of the universe. But He is not a dictator who imposes His will on us. He wants us to serve Him freely. That is why He expects His children to ask Him to reign. 'May your kingdom come,' means, 'I believe, Lord, that You are reigning, I long to see the world obeying Your laws, and I am ready to obey You in all things.'

'Thy will be done'

This request illustrates clearly the difference between Christian prayer and pagan prayer. The Christian prays so as to seek God's will, whereas the pagan prays to change the will of his god. He wants his own will to be done. The Christian may ask God to grant his wishes, but all Christian prayer should be first and foremost sincerely seeking the will of God.

'On earth as it is in heaven'

These few words are the conclusion of these first three requests. They explain that we would like the name of God to be hallowed, His will to be done and His kingdom to come on earth in the *same way* as in heaven, that is, perfectly. What we desire is the establishment of the kingdom of God.

'Give us this day our daily bread'

This fourth request teaches us to wait on God for all that is necessary for living. It is so easy to believe that God owes us food, clothing and everything that we need. God owes us nothing. We are nothing but lost sinners. It is in love that He takes care of us. In asking for our daily bread, (daily means 'today's') we acknowledge that if it were not for the love of God we could die of hunger.

'Forgive us our debts, as we also have forgiven our debtors'

With these words, we pray for the grace of God. We ask God to forget the evil that we have done. But we can only ask this favour on one condition; we must forget the evil which others have done to us. In this, Jesus shows the necessity of understanding what forgiveness is (Matthew 18:21–35). It is only as we ourselves forgive, that we can understand what forgiveness is and receive it from God.

'Do not lead us into temptation, but deliver us from evil'

We must not think, because of this request, that God tempts us. On the contrary, we are told, 'Let no one say when he is tempted, "I am being tempted by God"; for God cannot be tempted by evil, and He Himself does not tempt any one' (James 1:13).

However God allows us to live in a world full of temptations. We must be His witnesses in this world. But if God Himself does not deliver us, there is no hope of our overcoming temptation.

'For Thine is the kingdom, and the power, and the glory, forever. Amen'

The conclusion of this prayer is a clear affirmation of our faith in God. We declare with assurance that we pray to God because only He has power. He is the only King. We give glory to Him alone. The word, 'Amen,' means, 'It is true.' This word emphasizes the necessity of truly believing what we say in our prayers.

Serving God

Serving God begins with prayer. But we must serve God in all that we do. The Ten Commandments which God gave to Moses for His people explain to us the way in which God wants to be served. We must remember that the people of Israel had just come out of Egypt where they had been slaves. Similarly, the moment a person becomes a Christian, he also is released from the bondage of Satan. Like the people of Israel therefore, he needs to learn to live by different customs. The Ten Commandments are like a highway code for those who are walking in God's way. The first part, comprising the first four commandments, speaks of our relationship to God.

The first four commandments

'I am the Lord your God, who brought you out of the land of Egypt, out of the house of slavery. You shall have no other gods before Me' (Exodus 20:2–3).

This first commandment shows clearly that it is impossible to serve God lightly, that is, without giving Him our whole-hearted attention. Man needs to have a god. When he is not led by the Word of the Creator, he must have someone or something else to guide him. For some, it may be their fetish, for others money, an easy life or many other things. Now the first lesson that a

Christian must learn is that God wants to be the only Master: 'No one can serve two masters; for either he will hate the one and love the other, or he will hold to one and despise the other. You cannot serve God and mammon' (Matthew 6:24). When a Christian becomes cold, the cause is always the same: he has let himself be led away to serve another god. This may be mammon, the god of riches.

> 'You shall not make for yourself an idol, or any likeness of what is in heaven above or on the earth beneath or in the water under the earth. You shall not worship them or serve them; for I the Lord your God, am a jealous God, visiting the iniquity of the fathers on the children, on the third and the fourth generations of those who hate Me, but showing lovingkindness to thousands, to those who love Me and keep My commandments' (Exodus 20:4–6).

This second commandment is an explanation of the first. It condemns the worship of idols and fetishes. But we can be idolatrous without possessing or serving gods of wood or iron. It is very convenient to trust in human ideas which describe God differently from the Bible. It is so easy to let our imagination run wild and to believe in a god who conforms to our own ideas. The intellectual who puts his confidence in human wisdom can be as idolatrous as the illiterate worshipper of fetishes. This commandment also teaches that one does not mock God without incurring His curse. He allows the consequences of sin to be suffered for several generations. But He promises His mercy to thousands, to all those who love Him and keep His commandments.

> 'You shall not take the name of the Lord your God in vain, for the Lord will not leave him unpunished who takes His name in vain' (Exodus 20:7).

We are encouraged to pray, 'Hallowed be Thy name,' and so let us beware of mixing the name of God with worldly things which bear the mark of sin. Every time a Christian pronounces the name of God without telling the whole truth, he takes His name in vain. It is very serious to swear in the name of God. That is why Jesus said, 'But let your statement be, "Yes, yes" or "No, no"; and anything beyond these is of evil' (Matthew 5:37).

In addition, the Christian bears the name of Christ, and therefore of God. When he acts badly, he takes the name of God in vain. There was a Christian who used often to cross the frontier without being searched by the customs officers. They trusted him. One day a new officer searched him and discovered that he was carrying foreign currency which it was forbidden to take through without permission. They took the money from him saying, 'Now we know that the Christians' God is no stronger than the god of the pagans.' This Christian brought disgrace on the name of God. What a great sin!

> *'Remember the sabbath day, to keep it holy. Six days you shall labour and do all your work, but the seventh day is a sabbath of the Lord your God; in it you shall not do any work, you or your son or your daughter, your male or your female servant or your cattle or your sojourner who stays with you. For in six days the Lord made the heavens and the earth, the sea and all that is in them, and rested on the seventh day; therefore the Lord blessed the sabbath day and made it holy'* (Exodus 20:8–11).

All the commandments must be observed by Christians. But this one must first of all be explained by the work which Jesus Christ accomplished on the earth. The absolute rest of the sabbath foretold the perfect rest which Jesus Christ gives by His death and resurrection. The seventh day, the sabbath, was a picture. It taught the Israelites that, as you rest completely one day in seven from everything that tires your body, so one day you will find rest of heart, a perfect rest which will never end. As the Epistle to the Hebrews declares, 'There remains therefore a sabbath rest for the people of God. For the one who has entered His rest has himself also rested from his works, as God did from His' (Hebrews 4:9–10).

Since Jesus came to accomplish what the sabbath foretold, it would be unnecessary to continue to observe that day; it would even, in a way, be despising Christ's work. On the contrary, what we must now declare is that Jesus has come. His resurrection from the dead is the proof that He has conquered death. It is the resurrection that we must celebrate. The sabbath, Saturday, the last day of the week, foretold salvation to come; Sunday the first day of the week, recalls the victory of Jesus on Easter morning. The two days speak of the work of Jesus: one foretells it, the other reminds us of it. Sunday is not a new sabbath, a new law, but it is a day set apart for meditation on the Word of God, for remembering the resurrection. That is why the first Christians spontaneously observed this day as a festival consecrated to the praise of the Saviour (1 Corinthians 16:2).

The institution of the sabbath also teaches that God wants His children to honour Him in doing 'all their work'. Laziness, contempt for work, easy-going attitudes, and disorder are highly displeasing to the Lord who created the world in its perfection.

Finally, the sabbath underlines the necessity for taking rest. While God wants to see us working heartily (Colossians 3:23), He does not want work to become a new idol.

Jesus summed up these first four commandments in these words: 'You shall love the Lord your God with all your heart, and with all your soul, and with all your mind. This is the great and foremost commandment' (Matthew 22:37–38).

The Christian and his fellow man

Love for one's fellow man

The relationship of the Christian with his God is first of all a relationship of love. That is why Jesus adds to the 'great and foremost commandment', 'And a second is like it, "You shall love your neighbour as yourself" ' (Matthew 22:39).

This commandment to love one's neighbour sums up the second part of the Law (Romans 13:8–10), the last six commandments. It is also the result of love for God. In fact, the apostle John states, 'If some one says, "I love God," and hates his brother, he is a liar; for the one who does not love his brother whom he has seen, cannot love God whom he has not seen' (1 John 4:20).

Love for our fellow man is a proof that we love God. As a flame proves that there is fire, so love for one's neighbour shows one's love for God (Matthew 25:31–46). But how can we love our neighbour? Love is not expressed only in feelings or words. John continues, 'Little children, let us not love with word or with tongue, but in deed and truth' (1 John 3:18).

It is by our actions, by our whole life, that this love should be demonstrated. The commandments of the Law of Moses teach us love for our fellow men in a very practical way, which we can easily understand.

The last six commandments

'Honour your father and your mother, that your days may be prolonged in the land which the Lord your God gives you' (Exodus 20:12).

We owe our life to our parents. They deserve to be

respected and honoured. We must do all in our power to
see that they are happy, sheltered from poverty,
surrounded with affection, respect and attention.
However, that does not mean that parents who live with
their children have the right to order them about in
everything. The Bible also says, 'A man shall leave his
father and his mother, and shall cleave to his wife'
(Genesis 2:24).

Unpleasant scenes between daughters and mothers-in-
law do not help to make parents happy. It is often
necessary for the good of each party, that the son should
provide a home for his parents at a little distance. Good
relationships are a necessary part of the honour due to
parents.

This commandment concludes with a promise. Where
parents are honoured, happiness grows, and people may
even live longer! God is pleased to bless a family where
harmony reigns. But where there are scenes and discord,
God does not wish to prolong life and give further
opportunities for sin.

'You shall not murder' (Exodus 20:13).

Let us hear how Jesus Himself explains this
commandment.

'You have heard that the ancients were told, "You shall
not commit murder" and "Whoever commits murder
shall be liable to the court." But I say to you that every
one who is angry with his brother shall be guilty before
the court; and whoever shall say to his brother,
"Raca," shall be guilty before the supreme court; and
whoever shall say, "You fool" shall be guilty enough to
go into the hell of fire' (Matthew 5:21–22).

This sixth commandment is not only about killing the
body but also the harm that can be done to someone's
reputation. All anger and all insults come under this
condemnation. Each time we despise someone's name,
there is a sense in which we kill him by heaping scorn and
hatred on him. 'Do not commit murder,' means 'Do
nothing and say nothing that can harm your neighbour,'

that is, 'Do him good' (Romans 13:10).

'You shall not commit adultery' (Exodus 20:14).

Jesus also gave a very valuable explanation of this
commandment: 'You have heard that it was said, "You
shall not commit adultery"; but I say to you, that every
one who looks on a woman to lust for her has committed
adultery with her already in his heart' (Matthew 5:27–28).

Who can feel himself blameless before these words?
Any sexual relationship outside of marriage is adultery.
Elsewhere, this sin is called by other names (1 Corinthians
6:18; Romans 1:24). Paul often speaks of unchastity or
impurity. This sin is not in itself any more serious than
any other. But there are two people involved and the
serious consequences are irreparable. This is why the
Christian should have a horror of it.

First of all there are the consequences. How many
disastrous pregnancies there are, how many unfortunate
children who have no parents to take care of them! How
many broken homes, lies and even crimes because of one
moment of pleasure! Ordinary common sense, therefore,
is enough to condemn adultery.

The Bible adds another striking reason; it is impossible
to undo the deed. A thief can give back what he has
stolen, but what can a man do when he has abused a
woman? (Proverbs 6:29–35.)

Besides, the whole of Scripture shows us that marital
love is a gift which God gave to man when He created
him: 'A man shall cleave to his wife; and they shall
become one flesh' (Genesis 2:24).

The physical union is a gift, a very precious gift
(Ecclesiastes 9:9). We must take great care of it, and hold
it in great honour. It is the most beautiful expression of
the love between a man and his wife (Proverbs 5:15–21).
Every time that this seventh commandment is violated,
this wonderful gift is dragged in the mud. It is polluted,
treated like a cheap toy, a simple instrument of self-
gratification.

When you give a very precious gift to your child, you
want him to take care of it. What will you think if your

child mistreats your gift and drags it in the mud? In the same way, God is gravely offended by unchastity.

Finally Paul declares to the Corinthians, 'Do you not know that your body is a temple of the Holy Spirit who is in you, whom you have from God, and that you are not your own?' (1 Corinthians 6:19).

When you want to honour an important visitor, you lodge him in a lovely house, clean and arranged to suit his taste. God tells us that he detests adultery. Since He lives in us by the Holy Spirit, we cannot give our body over to sin, which He hates. Anyone who gives himself to unchastity offends the Holy Spirit.

'You shall not steal' (Exodus 20:15).

Love for one's fellow man demands that we respect him, and do him no harm. What is more, it requires us to respect all that he possesses. There is a way of stealing from one's neighbour by not taking care of his things. The workman who takes no care of his employer's tools or materials is not fulfilling this commandment. The child who wastes his parents' money is not acting out of love for them. The neighbour who does not give back what he has borrowed is breaking this commandment.

The Christian must show his love for his fellow man by respecting what belongs to him. The commandment condemns all dishonest business and all excessive profit making.

'You shall not bear false witness against your neighbour' (Exodus 20:16).

Satan is called 'the father of lies' (John 8:44). Each time a Christian does not tell the truth, he stops being like God and resembles Satan! False witness is a terrible way of hurting one's neighbour. Someone who acts as a witness tells what he knows. When he invents or distorts the truth for his own profit or out of fear, he commits a very grave sin; he is allowing Satan to speak through his mouth.

In a certain village, they could not settle a dispute, so someone suggested that they should fetch a Christian witness. Then they could be sure that he was telling the truth. Was that not a good testimony? In the world of trade, in administration, wherever he is, the Christian should be known for his straight dealings and his habit of telling only the truth. Tax returns, birth certificates or other documents should never be changed with the intention of misleading anyone. Only the strict truth is worthy of the name of Christian.

'You shall not covet your neighbour's house; you shall not covet your neighbour's wife or his male servant or his female servant or his ox or his donkey or anything that belongs to your neighbour' (Exodus 20:17).

This commandment shows us where we need to attack sin. Covetousness is at the root of sin and has to be pulled out. Without covetousness there is no theft, no adultery, no murder, no lies. The evil desires which fill our heart have to be carefully rooted out.

Let us first ask God in prayer to deliver us from the evil desires that pollute our heart. Then we must take action and deliberately turn away from anything that could awaken the covetousness dormant within us. We must flee from bad company, evil places, and we must avoid idleness, laziness and carelessness (Proverbs 7). Jesus, in His sermon on the mount, admirably summed up these six commandments in a very practical way: 'Whatever you want others to do for you, do so for them; for this is the Law and the Prophets' (Matthew 7:12).

In fact, you only need to put yourself in the place of your fellow man, to act towards him with love. That is exactly what it means to love your neighbour as yourself.

17

The Christian and material things

Beware of the trap!

In the world, material things mean everything. Money, clothes, the car and food become real idols. These things are useful, and often necessary, but the Christian should not think of them as of first importance. Jesus said to us, 'For all these things the Gentiles eagerly seek' (Matthew 6:32).

Many Christians who have been set free from their sins by Jesus Christ have let themselves gradually slide back into a worldly way of life. Their love for God has burnt dim and gone out. Their joy in serving Him has disappeared. Why? They have yielded too large a place in their heart to the god of money (Matthew 13:22; 1 Timothy 6:7–11). In this way material things can become snares. Let us be wise, and not be led away by them.

God looks after His children

'Your Father knows what you need, before you ask Him' (Matthew 6:8).

These words of Jesus mean two things. Firstly, food is a necessity for the life of our body and clothes for life in society. God does not want Christians to live in poverty (Matthew 6:19–34). Would He, who feeds the birds of the air and clothes with splendour even the grass of the fields, want His children to be badly fed and clothed? It is as wrong to despise lovely things when God gives them to us as it is to give them the first place in our hearts (1 Timothy 6:17).

Secondly, since we know that God takes care of us, our one concern should be to serve Him with all our hearts.

As we have seen, the service of God includes our work (see chapter 15). So it is not a question of giving way to laziness under the pretext that God takes care of us! The apostle Paul said, 'If anyone will not work, neither let him eat' (2 Thessalonians 3:10).

Serving God first

'But seek first His kingdom, and His righteousness; and all these things shall be added to you' (Matthew 6:33).

The Christian no longer lives for himself but for his Lord. Instead of worrying about his own needs, he is concerned about the needs of the kingdom of God. The first book of Kings (chapter 17:8–16) tells us the story of a woman who had nothing to eat. But the prophet Elijah commanded her, with the little she had left, to make a loaf for him, the man of God. The woman obeyed. The oil in the jar and the flour in the bowl never ran out all the time the famine lasted. Are we ready to put at God's disposal all that we possess—our strength, our intelligence, our money, our car, our house and our time? The person who seeks first the kingdom and righteousness of God, does all in his power to oppose injustice. Within the limits of his means, he helps out those who lack basic necessities: 'But whoever has the world's goods, and beholds his brother in need and closes his heart against him, how does the love of God abide in him?' (1 John 3:17).

If we seek first the kingdom and righteousness of God, He will give us what we need in abundance. God may put us to the test, as He did with Job. He can take back all that He has given us. When that happens, let us be able to say with Job, 'The Lord gave and the Lord has taken away. Blessed be the name of the Lord' (Job 1:21).

Our attitude to material things shows what our love for God and our neighbour is worth (Malachi 3:10). Indeed Jesus told us, 'Where your treasure is, there will your heart be also' (Matthew 6:21).

18
The Christian and the world

Up till now we have studied the ways in which our love for God should translate itself into practical living. After having spoken about our relationship with our fellow man and our attitude towards material things, it remains for us to see what the Bible says about community life—the Christian and the world, the Christian and the state and the Christian and the local church.

What is the world?

This word occurs very often in the Bible, and we need to understand it. It has several different meanings. We will consider the two most important ones.

1. God's creation

The prophet Jeremiah declared, 'He ... established the world by His wisdom' (Jeremiah 10:12).

This text and many others concern God's creation. God Himself found it very good (Genesis 1:31). It suffered because of sin (Romans 8:20-22), but it is still subject to the laws appointed by God (Psalm 148:6-8). The Christian's calling in the world as created by God, was clearly expressed at the moment of creation: 'And God created man in His own image, in the image of God He created him; male and female He created them. And God blessed them; and God said to them, "Be fruitful and multiply, and fill the earth, and subdue it" ' (Genesis 1:27-28).

This text reminds us of the biblical basis for the family, but it also establishes the commission given to man to subdue the earth. 'Subdue' means to bring something under control. With the intelligence which God has given him, man must try to understand the laws of creation (science) and to master the forces of nature (technology). The Christian who is faithful to this calling glorifies his Creator. That is why work and study should not be despised by the Christian, but carried out conscientiously for the glory of God.

2. The enemy of God

The apostle John declared, 'Do not love the world, nor the things in the world' (1 John 2:15).

Here it is no longer a question of the world as God's creation, but of the world in revolt against God (James 4:4). These two aspects of the world are very clearly linked and this is what makes the life of a Christian disciple more complicated. The Christian is constantly in danger of becoming caught up in the world which is the enemy of God, or of failing in his calling as a witness by withdrawing too far from the world. But Jesus does not want to see His disciples shutting themselves off from the world. Praying for them, He said, 'I do not ask Thee to take them out of the world, but to keep them from the evil one' (John 17:15).

The calling of the Christian in this world, which is hostile to God, is to be 'the light of the world', proclaiming by his acts and his words the good news of Jesus Christ (Matthew 28:19). The presence of disciples in this world is like the action of salt (Matthew 5:13): it combats decay and gives a pleasant taste. By his testimony the Christian is called to fight against evil and show to the world the true meaning of its existence.

Christian liberty

The disciple of Jesus Christ is free (John 8:36). He is no longer a slave of sin like the citizens of the world which is hostile to God. He has received strength to overcome temptations and to act out of love. The apostle Paul expresses very clearly what this liberty means: 'All things are lawful, but not all things are profitable. All things are lawful, but not all things edify. Let no one seek his own good, but that of his neighbour' (1 Corinthians 10:23–24).

Christian liberty is not a freedom for self, but a freedom for others (Galatians 5:13–14). In his choice of what he eats or what he drinks, the Christian thinks first of all of the interests of others. He should not ask himself whether something is forbidden or allowed, but, 'Is it for the good of my neighbour?' That is why the apostle Paul declares, 'Therefore, if food causes my brother to stumble, I will never eat meat again, that I might not cause my brother to stumble' (1 Corinthians 8:13).

In the apostle Paul's time, the problem was particularly about meat sacrificed to idols. Nowadays a Christian who is truly free might deprive himself of, say, wine, tobacco or some legitimate amusement because of love for his neighbour.

Sin is not in objects

Sin is in the use we make of things, not in the things themselves. A machete knife is a very useful tool, but if someone uses it to kill his neighbour, it becomes an instrument of sin. Do we condemn the knife, or the man who is holding it? There is no sin in smoke, but someone who is a slave of tobacco is committing a sin, because he despises the freedom which Jesus Christ gives him. (We could also add that smoking is bad for one's health in the long run and it is therefore wise to abstain from it.) A person who dances is not sinning, but some dances arouse carnal desires. A man or woman who goes in for dancing runs the risk of falling into immorality and of causing another person to sin as well.

The Bible does not forbid the use of these things. It exhorts us for our own and for our neighbour's good, to be sober. These things must not be placed under a form of taboo. But, just as in a time of drought it is dangerous to play with fire, so it may be wise to abstain from something which is in itself legitimate in order to avoid awakening the covetousness which is latent in us.

Above all, let us beware of judging others

We must beware of judging people who do things from which we abstain (Romans 14:13). The spirit of judgement is inspired by pride, which when it penetrates even the spiritual life, is perhaps the worst of sins. The faithful disciple acts only out of conviction, for he knows that 'whatever is not from faith is sin' (Romans 14:23), and his only concern is to glorify his God according to the exhortation of the apostle Paul: 'Whether, then, you eat or drink or whatever you do, do all to the glory of God' (1 Corinthians 10:31).

19

The Christian and the state

The dual nationality of the Christian

Since he lives in this world, the Christian remains a citizen
of his country, his province, his town or his village. He
does not stop belonging to his country because he
belongs to the kingdom of heaven. So the Christian
possesses a dual nationality. How can he be a good citizen
of his country without betraying the kingdom of God,
and how can he 'seek first the kingdom and
righteousness of God' and still remain a good citizen of
his earthly country? Jesus replied in a few words to those
who came to test him with a similar question: 'Render to
Caesar (the state) the things that are Caesar's (the state's);
and to God the things that are God's' (Matthew 22:21).

By giving the state what he owes it, the Christian will be
a good citizen. His loyalty to the authorities forms part of
his testimony.

The existence of the state is intended by God

Like the family, the state forms part of the order
established in the world as God created it (Romans
13:1–2).

'By me kings reign, and rulers decree justice. By me
princes rule, and nobles, all who judge rightly' (Proverbs
8:15–16).

It is the wisdom of God which is speaking here. The
state is ordained by God so that order and peace reign in
the world. Unfortunately, because the state is made up of
men, it is also tainted by sin. But in spite of that, it retains
its powers. It is responsible for the maintenance of
political, economic and social order (1 Peter 2:14;

Romans 13:3–4). It is ordered by God to punish evil doers
and to collect taxes (Romans 13:6–7).

Respect due to authorities

The apostle Paul declares, 'Let every person be in
subjection to the governing authorities. For there is no
authority except from God, and those which exist are
established by God' (Romans 13:1).

It is from God Himself that the magistrates derive their
power. That is why Christians, even more than the
people of this world, must obey the authorities. They
must be right with the law. The Christian cannot allow
himself to cheat. The papers for his car must be in order,
his tax return must be accurate. Also his marriage must
be legally registered.

The limits of obedience due to the authorities

We owe respect to the authorities in all matters which
concern them. But in the spiritual realm, the state has no
authority. We must give to Caesar (to the state) what is
due to Caesar, and to God, what is due to God. When the
authorities wanted to prevent Peter and the apostles from
speaking of their faith in Jesus Christ, they replied, 'We
must obey God rather than men' (Acts 5:29).

Prayer for the authorities

We know that God is sovereign. He is over all things. The
authorities have been appointed by Him.

In the conviction that God can do everything, we must
pray for all those who bear the heavy responsibilities of
running the state: 'First of all, then, I urge that entreaties
and prayers, petitions and thanksgivings, be made on
behalf of all men, for kings and all who are in authority,
in order that we may lead a tranquil and quiet life in all
godliness and dignity' (1 Timothy 2:1–2).

The Christian should take an interest in the affairs of his
nation

As we have seen, the Bible exhorts the Christian to be an
excellent citizen by his obedience to the authorities. If a
Christian really desires the good of his nation, he must be
interested in his nation's affairs. He should show his
interest by voting, and by taking part in elections.

The Christian and politics

Can a Christian belong to a political party? Can he
become a statesman? If the party respects his religious
convictions, there is nothing to stop him.

The Bible gives several examples of men of God who
were at the same time remarkable statesmen. Not only
the kings of Israel—David, Solomon, Hezekiah—but
many other men held positions of authority in pagan
countries, like Joseph, for example (Genesis 41–47). He
maintained a wonderful testimony at the court of
Pharaoh, king of Egypt. Certainly, a Christian who is
called to exercise this sort of power comes up against
tremendous temptations. He has to face almost
insurmountable problems. But a Christian can accept
such responsibility if he has the firm conviction that God
is calling him to it, for His glory and for the good of his
fellow men.

Church leaders and politics

We should note, however, that a pastor or evangelist
should never accept political office, for wherever leaders
of churches have been involved in politics, confusion has
resulted. The pastor can no more meddle in affairs of
state than the state can intervene in spiritual matters. The
role of the state is to establish and maintain order in
society. The role of the church and of its leaders is to
proclaim the kingdom of God, which is not of this world.

Both ministries are instituted by God, but their nature is so different that they cannot be carried out at the same time by the same person.

The Christian and the local church

The local church is an embassy

The local church is not just another society. Its members do not meet together for their own benefit. They meet together to please their God and to proclaim His Word. The local church is an embassy of the kingdom of God in the world. All Christians are therefore ambassadors (2 Corinthians 5:20). The example of an ambassador helps us to understand how the Christian should behave in the world and in the local church.

Participation in the life of the local church

An ambassador must have a thorough knowledge of the country which he represents. That is why the Christian must learn to know the kingdom of God by studying the Bible. But personal study is not enough. Whenever he can, a Christian should join a group of evangelical believers. The local church is a refuge in the midst of the world. The Christian really can find there, in brotherly love, in meditation on the Word of God and in praise, the strength which he needs. That is why it is written: 'Not forsaking our own assembling together, as is the habit of some, but encouraging one another' (Hebrews 10:25).

A pastor was once visiting a Christian who no longer came to the services. The man explained to his pastor that he still read the Bible regularly. He did not see any need to join the church community. The pastor made no reply. It was winter and a coal fire was burning in the grate. The pastor approached the fire and took out a burning piece of coal. The man watched him in amazement. After a few moments the coal stopped glowing. It became cold. Suddenly the man exclaimed, 'I see! A Christian becomes cold when he does not participate in the life of the church.' The very next Sunday, this Christian set off for chapel again.

The responsibilities of the Christian in the church

We do not join a church only to receive but also to contribute. It is in proportion as we give that we receive (Mark 4:24–25). Each Christian can contribute what he has. Someone who is a good singer can use his voice in the service of God. Someone who knows how to speak or to lead in worship can use his gifts for the glory of God and not for the glory of his own name (Romans 12:6–8). Everyone without exception must find some work to do in the church. Even the person who tends the garden or cleans the chapel is doing something useful: 'As each one has received a special gift, employ it in serving one another, as good stewards of the manifold grace of God' (1 Peter 4:10).

The collection

Among the gifts which a Christian possesses are his material goods. But how should he offer them to God? The church is an embassy of the kingdom of God on earth and as such is responsible to make the name of God known to men. Church workers, pastors, evangelists, all those who devote all their time to a particular ministry, must live. It is a bad witness if they are badly clothed, badly housed or badly fed. What would people say about a country if the ambassador and his colleagues led a poor wretched life? Alas, this is too often the case among God's servants because Christians do not do their duty. It is true that poverty can also be a testimony in this world, where people think only of material things. But it is not right for a pastor or an evangelist to be poorer than the Christians who are supporting him. It is not enough to guarantee the salary of church workers. They must also be given the tools they need for their work. Transport is very expensive. Many evangelists never reach remote areas because of lack of money! Modern methods of evangelization are very effective, but they are also very expensive. Giving a part of one's goods to God's work is more than a duty; it is the privilege of putting one's money into the finest enterprise of all (Matthew 6:20).

In the Old Testament, the children of Israel had to give at least a tithe—a tenth of all that they earned (Leviticus 27:30). In the church, there is no law. No one is obliged to give anything, but the New Testament invites us to bring our offering to God: 'On the first day of every week, let each one of you put aside and save, as he may prosper' (1 Corinthians 16:2).

Our offering should be a token of our love for God. If we love someone, we give that person a special present. We give it joyfully. This is the spirit in which we should bring our offerings: 'Let each one do just as he has purposed in his heart; not grudgingly or under compulsion; for God loves a cheerful giver' (2 Corinthians 9:7).

If we give little, it is because we love little. God promises blessing to those who commit themselves to give of their goods. The prophet Malachi wrote, ' "Bring the whole tithe into the storehouse, so that there may be food in My house, and test Me now in this," says the Lord of hosts, "if I will not open for you the windows of heaven, and pour out for you a blessing until there is no more need" ' (Malachi 3:10).

Discipline

Too often a Christian is not a good ambassador for the kingdom of God in the world. He does not seize every opportunity to witness for Jesus Christ. Sometimes even, he may fall into sin. If Christians behave in the same way as worldly people, how can the world get to know Jesus Christ? 'You are the salt of the earth; but if the salt has become tasteless, how will it be made salty again? It is good for nothing any more, except to be thrown out and trampled under foot by men' (Matthew 5:13).

What would people think of an earthly country whose ambassador indulged in drunkenness, in taking other people's wives or daughters, or in making false declarations? He would destroy not only his own reputation, but that of his country as well.

That is why when a Christian falls into serious sin, he is asked to stop fulfilling his responsibilities for a time, and to stop coming to the Lord's Table. *This is not a punishment* but an action taken for three important reasons.

Firstly, by withdrawing from the person who has brought disgrace on the kingdom of God, the church shows openly that it disapproves of his conduct (1 Corinthians 5:11). All the countries of the world act in this way with regard to their ambassadors. If one of them behaves badly, he is called back. It is vital for the world to know that the church does not approve of those who behave badly.

Secondly, the one who has been the cause of a scandal must be put aside to permit him to reflect and repent (James 5:19). But it is in a spirit of love, with gentleness as well as firmness, that he will be made to see his error.

Finally, a person who behaves badly, and who perseveres in his sin, must not partake of the Lord's Supper, for the apostle Paul declares, 'Therefore whoever eats the bread or drinks the cup of the Lord in an unworthy manner, shall be guilty of the body and the blood of the Lord' (1 Corinthians 11:27).

Paul adds that several Christians in the Corinthian church had become ill. Some had even died because they had despised the Lord's Table (1 Corinthians 11:30). We may only approach the Lord's Table with a repentant heart. Anyone who partakes of the Lord's Supper while living in any form of sin, is a hypocrite.

How to practise discipline

The Bible also teaches how discipline should be practised.

Paul says to the Corinthians, 'But let a man examine himself' (1 Corinthians 11:28).

When someone has committed a serious sin, he himself should decide to abstain for a time from the Lord's Table, and from his responsibilities in the church. But when the one who has fallen persists in his sin, he cannot be allowed to take part in the activities of the church without being warned. Jesus Christ said, 'And if your brother sins, go and reprove him in private; if he listens to you, you have won your brother. But if he does not listen to you, take one or two more with you, so that by the mouth of two or three witnesses every fact may be confirmed. And if he refuses to listen to them, tell it to the church; and if he refuses to listen even to the church, let him be to you as a Gentile and a tax-gatherer' (Matthew 18:15–17).

This way of acting is inspired by Christian love. Indeed, Christian affairs should not be settled like those of worldly people. We must be very careful about the way we speak (James 3:1–12). Sin is too serious to be spoken of lightly. On the contrary, it should make us deeply sad.

Returning to the Lord's Table, and taking up responsibilities again

When someone has had to be put aside, the others must pray for him, and wait lovingly until he repents. It is not necessary that he should be deprived of the Lord's Table for long. As soon as he has abandoned his sinful way of life, he can take part again in the fellowship of the Lord's Supper. If he had important responsibilities in the church, if he was an elder, or preacher, he would not take up his duties again immediately. But if he bears a good testimony, the church will give them back to him as soon as it is satisfied that the world round about has also been witness of his repentance. It is not the time factor which is important, but the sincerity of the repentance.

Let us be good ambassadors for the kingdom of God in this world. Let us fulfil well our responsibilities in the local church. May God be able to find us faithful in all things.

Offices in the local church

For the smooth running of the local church, and so that the Word of God be correctly proclaimed, various offices have been instituted. It is the Holy Spirit who qualifies certain Christians who are called to a particular office, that is to say to a particular form of service: 'And He gave some as apostles, and some as prophets, and some as evangelists, and some as pastors and teachers, for the equipping of the saints for the work of service, to the building up of the body of Christ' (Ephesians 4:11–12).

Those to whom God has entrusted some form of office in the local church have been given a very important task: that of edifying the church. The apostle Paul, in his Epistles to Timothy and Titus, describes the qualities of the servant of God (Titus 1:5–9; 1 Timothy 3). As well as having a good reputation, the one who aspires to responsibility must be capable of *teaching* the Word of God. That is why it is absolutely necessary that a servant of God should have received a solid training. He must have a deep knowledge of the Bible, and of all that touches on his ministry.

Conclusion

There are two sorts of servants: those who wait for their master's orders, without doing anything, and those who know their master so well that they always know what must be done and do it! Is it not the same for God's servants, that is to say, for all Christians? That is why it is so important to know God.

But God is not only a Master; He wants above all to be our Father. Do we want to be His sons? It is very rare for a master to entrust to his servants delicate missions or important responsibilities, but God who is the Father of those who serve Him, entrusts to His sons the task of representing Him in this world, of being His ambassadors. What an honour that is! How are we fulfilling this charge? What do the people think who see our lives? What idea do they have of the kingdom of God?

Do we really seek first the kingdom of God? In our family life and in our work, are we always peaceable and joyful, ready to serve?

It is as impossible to serve God without knowing Him as it is to claim to know Him and not serve Him. That is why we must know God if we are to serve Him better.

May this simple book help those whom God has called to the new life, to be the salt of the earth and the light of the world.

Appendix
Division of the Chapters into Lessons and Questions

PART 1 THE MAJOR DOCTRINES

Chapter 1 Revelation

Lesson 1: (pages 4–6)

Can we know God?
Natural revelation
Spoken revelation
Written revelation
Revelation in Jesus Christ

Questions:
1. What is the only source from which to draw Christian doctrine?
2. Can man discover God by his own efforts?
3. Why does natural revelation leave man without excuse?
4. Why is spoken revelation insufficient?
5. Why did God ordain that His Word should be written?
6. Why is Jesus Christ called the Word?

Lesson 2: (pages 6–7)

The inspiration of the Bible
The Bible is the Word of God
The Word of God is truth
Science and the Bible

Questions:
1. Why did God see fit to use men to write His Word?

2. Why is it important to believe that the Bible is the Word of God?
3. Are there practical consequences which follow from believing that the Bible is the Word of God and that it tells the truth? If so, what are they?
4. How should we answer those who claim that there are contradictions between science and the Bible?

Chapter 2 The doctrine of God

Lesson 3: (pages 8–10)

   A word of warning
   There is only one God
   The mystery of the Trinity
   The Trinity and the experience of salvation

Questions:
1. Why is it dangerous to depict God visually?
2. What are the practical consequences of believing that there is only one God?
3. Explain how it is not a contradiction to believe that the one God is in three Persons.
4. What do each of the three Persons of the Trinity do for the salvation of men?
5. According to John 14:26, what do the three Persons of the Trinity do?

Lesson 4: (pages 10–13)

   God is eternal
   God is all-powerful
   God is everywhere
   God knows everything

Questions:
1. What does the word 'eternal' mean?
2. What is the importance of believing that God is really all-powerful?

3. What is the connection between the justice of God and the fact that He is everywhere?
4. Why is it that faith in the God who knows everything encourages us to leave to Him the direction of our lives?

Lesson 5: (pages 13–14)

God is love
God is just
God is holy

Questions:
1. What is the difference between God, the Creator, as portrayed in traditional African religions and the God of the Bible?
2. How is the love of God towards men shown? Give four proofs of His love.
3. What is the difference between the mercy of God and human pity?
4. Explain how the love and the justice of God are not contradictory, but in Jesus Christ the two go hand-in-hand.
5. What is the importance for the Christian life of knowing that God is holy?

Chapter 3 The doctrine of the Son

Lesson 6: (pages 15–17)

The importance of this doctrine
The person of Jesus Christ
The names the Bible gives to Jesus Christ

Questions:
1. Is it possible to know and meet God without His revelation in Jesus Christ?
2. For which ministries was Jesus anointed?

3. Why did Jesus have to be Son of Man and Son of God at the same time?
4. What does the expression 'Son of God' definitely not mean?

Lesson 7: (pages 17–20)

The life of Jesus Christ
The birth of Jesus
The baptism of Jesus
The temptation of Jesus
The miracles of Jesus
The teaching of Jesus

Questions:
1. What is the significance of the fact that Jesus' birth was miraculous?
2. What are the differences between Jesus' baptism and our baptism?
3. What does the story of the temptation of Jesus teach us?
4. What is the difference between the miracles of Jesus and those of His disciples?
5. In what different ways did Jesus give His teaching?

Lesson 8: (pages 20–22)

The condemnation of Jesus
The death of Jesus
The resurrection of Jesus

Questions:
1. Why did the Jews hate Jesus?
2. Was Jesus obliged to give His life?
3. How was it that Jesus put His own teaching into practice on the cross?
4. Read Isaiah 53 and say why it is said of Isaiah that he was a fifth evangelist.
5. Why do we know that the resurrection of Jesus is a historic fact and not an illusion on the part of the disciples?

Lesson 9: (pages 22–23)

The nature of the resurrection of Jesus
The resurrection of Jesus is a promise
The ascension of Jesus

Questions:
1. Was the body of Jesus after His resurrection the same as during His earthly life, and why?
2. What does the word 'incorruptible' mean?
3. Read 1 Corinthians 15:12–21 and say why the doctrine of the resurrection of Jesus is the foundation of the Christian faith.
4. What would the death of Jesus mean if He had not risen from the dead?
5. Why was it better for us (John 16:7) that Jesus should go back to heaven?

Lesson 10: (pages 24–26)

The work of Jesus Christ
Redemption
Atonement
Justification
Reconciliation
Forgiveness
Grace
Sanctification

Questions:
1. To whom was the price of our redemption, that is, the very life of Jesus Christ, paid?
2. What is the difference between the sacrifice of atonement and most of the sacrifices ordained by the traditional African religions?
3. What is the difference between the verb 'to justify' as it is used in our everyday language, and the verb 'to justify' as it is used in the Bible?
4. Why is grace a free gift?
5. What is the basis on which we can be reconciled to God?

6. What is the difference between justification and sanctification?

Chapter 4 The doctrine of the Holy Spirit

Lesson 11: (pages 27–28)

Who is the Holy Spirit?
The Holy Spirit is a Person
The Holy Spirit is God
The work of the Holy Spirit

Questions:
1. Why does the Bible say of the Spirit of God that He is *holy*?
2. Why is it important to believe that the Holy Spirit is a Person and not simply a power or an influence?
3. How do we know that the Holy Spirit is a Person?
4. Why is it important to believe that the Holy Spirit is God?
5. What does the Holy Spirit do?

Lesson 12: (pages 28–31)

The fruit and the gifts of the Holy Spirit
The fulness of the Holy Spirit
The sin against the Holy Spirit

Questions:
1. How is the presence of the Holy Spirit seen when He is living in a believer?
2. Read Matthew 7:15–20 and show how Galatians 5:22 complements this passage.
3. What is the difference between the fruit of the Spirit (Galatians 5:22) and the gifts of the Spirit (1 Corinthians 12:8–10)?
4. What is the sin against the Holy Spirit?
5. Would a person who had committed this sin be concerned about his salvation?

6. Explain the difference between the two aspects of the
   fulness of the Holy Spirit.

Chapter 5 The doctrine of man

Lesson 13: (pages 32–33)

> What is man?
> The origin of man
> Man is a responsible being
> The purpose of man's life

Questions:
1. Why is it that only the Bible can really answer the
   question, 'What is man'?
2. What practical consequences follow from faith in God
   as Creator?
3. What does the word 'responsible' mean?
4. What is the main difference between men and
   animals?
5. What is the purpose of man's life?

Lesson 14: (pages 33–35)

> The Fall
> The results of the Fall
> Redemption

Questions:
1. Why were Adam and Eve given a choice?
2. Why was it that the knowledge of good and evil, which
   the tree would give, seemed desirable to Adam and
   Eve?
3. Why do all the descendants of Adam and Eve suffer
   the consequences of sin?
4. When will redemption become effective in every area
   of life?

Chapter 6 The doctrine of the church

Lesson 15: (pages 36–37)

The church is the people of God
Definition

Questions:
1. What is the difference between the people of Israel and the church?
2. What does the word 'church' mean?
3. What do we understand by the term 'the invisible church'?
4. Why is the invisible church called 'the universal church'?

Lesson 16: (pages 37–39)

The church as the body of Christ
The church as the bride of Christ
The mission of the church

Questions:
1. What does the picture of the body teach us about the relationship of the church with Christ, and about the relationship of Christians with each other?
2. How does the picture of the body underline the unity and diversity of the church?
3. How can divisions between churches be avoided?
4. What does the picture of the bride teach us?
5. Why does Jesus still leave His church in the world?

Chapter 7 The doctrine of baptism and the Lord's Supper

Lesson 17: (pages 40–41)

Why baptism and the Lord's Supper?
Baptism is a sign of identity
Baptism and the work of Jesus Christ

Questions:
1. What is the difference between preaching by word and preaching by baptism and the Lord's Supper?
2. Why do we need water baptism?
3. If baptism is a sort of mark of identity, might it not possibly sometimes be a false mark? If so, when?
4. Who gives us the right to receive baptism, and why?

Lesson 18: (pages 42–43)

The Lord's Supper and the Passover
The Lord's Supper and fellowship
How we should take the Lord's Supper

Questions:
1. Explain the similarities between the Jewish Passover and the Lord's Supper.
2. Why is the Lord's Supper sometimes called 'communion'?
3. What conditions should we fulfil in order to partake of the Lord's Supper?
4. Why should we not neglect baptism and the Lord's Supper?

Chapter 8 The doctrine of the last things

Lesson 19: (pages 44–46)

What is there beyond death?
After death
The return of Jesus Christ
The judgement
The condemnation
Eternal salvation

Questions:
1. Why is it impossible for us to imagine life after death?
2. What happens to those who die before the return of Christ?

3. What extraordinary miracle will take place at the return of Jesus Christ?
4. According to Luke 12:47–48, will those who will be punished all receive the same punishment?
5. What should be the effect in the heart of the believer of the knowledge of the troubles which will come upon those who do not know God?
6. According to 1 Corinthians 3:15, what are the works which will merit a reward?

Chapter 9 The doctrine of angels

Lesson 20: (pages 47–49)

Who are the angels?
What do angels do?
Satan ·
Demons and evil spirits

Questions:
1. According to Hebrews 13:2, why could people have entertained angels without knowing it?
2. Why should we neither pray to, nor worship angels?
3. Can Satan do anything he wants?
4. Why should we avoid anything that has been involved with serving demons?

PART 2 HOW TO BECOME A CHRISTIAN

Chapter 10 Man can do nothing to save himself

Lesson 21: (pages 53–54)

Our actions have no merit
There is no salvation except in Jesus Christ

Questions:
1. Why is it impossible for us to do anything to earn salvation?
2. It is said, 'All religions are good provided people practise them sincerely.' Why is such a statement absolutely contrary to the gospel?
3. Why is it necessary for us that Jesus should come into and change our hearts?
4. Find some expressions which speak of the experience by which a person becomes a Christian.

Chapter 11 Faith

Lesson 22: (pages 55–57)

Faith is absolutely necessary for salvation
Definition of faith

Questions:
1. How does the Old Testament explain what faith is?
2. Is belief something that applies only to matters of religion?
3. What is the difference between faith and sight?
4. What example did Jesus leave us to help us understand what trustful faith is?
5. Why does the apostle James say that faith without works is dead?

Chapter 12 Conversion and repentance

Lesson 23: (pages 58–60)

What is conversion?
False conversions
What is repentance?
The signs of repentance

Questions:
1. Show the relationship between faith and conversion.
2. Read Matthew 13:1–23 and explain why some conversions do not last.
3. How is repentance a part of conversion?
4. Is repentance merely a change in a person's way of thinking?

Chapter 13 The new birth

Lesson 24: (pages 61–63)

What is the new birth?
Assurance of salvation
The old man and the new man
How can we overcome?

Questions:
1. What is the difference between conversion and the new birth?
2. Is it possible to be absolutely sure of one's salvation?
3. Why is the Christian life a battle?
4. How is it possible to know if a desire comes from the new man or the old man?

Part 3 WHAT THE CHRISTIAN LIFE MEANS IN PRACTICE

Chapter 14 What is the Christian life?

Lesson 25: (pages 67–69)

The true meaning of life re-discovered

The duty of a son
The aim of the Christian life

Questions:
1. What is the real purpose of life?
2. How does God want us to serve Him?
3. Why is the Law of God hard for certain Christians?
4. How can we be like God?

Chapter 15 The Christian before God

Lesson 26: (pages 70–72)

The Christian and prayer
The Lord's prayer:
'Our Father who art in heaven'

Questions:
1. Say why, according to Matthew 28:20, we can be sure that our prayers are heard?
2. According to Matthew 6:6–8, what are the two dangers which threaten our prayers?
3. Why does Jesus leave us a model prayer?
4. By what right are we able to call God our Father?
5. In the Lord's prayer the requests are arranged in a certain order. What does this teach us?

Lesson 27: (pages 72–73)

The Lord's prayer:
'Hallowed be Thy name'
'Thy kingdom come'
'Thy will be done'
'On earth as it is in heaven'

Questions:
1. How can a Christian hallow the name of God in his life?

2. Explain the difference between pagan prayer and Christian prayer.
3. Why does Jesus teach us to ask for the coming of the kingdom of God?
4. What do the words 'on earth as it is in heaven' mean?

Lesson 28: (pages 73–74)

The Lord's prayer:
'Give us this day our daily bread'
'Forgive us our debts ...'
'Do not lead us into temptation ...'
'For Thine is the kingdom ...'

Questions:
1. Why should we ask God for our daily food?
2. Why do we ask to be forgiven 'as we also have forgiven' others?
3. Is it possible for us to overcome temptation in our own strength?
4. Why does Jesus teach us to end our prayers by saying, 'Amen'?

Lesson 29: (pages 74–75)

Serving God
The first four commandments:
'I am the Lord your God ...'
'You shall not make for yourself an idol ...'

Questions:
1. Why do we need the commandments of God?
2. Is it possible for man not to worship any god at all?
3. What happens to a Christian who lets himself put his trust in a god other than the Lord?
4. Is it possible to be an idolater even without worshipping gods of wood or metal?

Lesson 30: (pages 75–77)

The first four commandments:
'You shall not take the name of the Lord your God in vain ...'
'Remember the sabbath day, to keep it holy ...'

Questions:
1. Give two ways in which someone can take the name of God in vain.
2. Why had God ordained the sabbath for the Jews?
3. Why do we no longer need to observe the seventh day of the week?
4. Why did the early Christians begin to observe Sunday?

Chapter 16 The Christian and his fellow man

Lesson 31: (pages 78–80)

Love for one's fellow man
The last six commandments:
'Honour your father and mother ...'
'You shall not murder'

Questions:
1. Explain how love for one's fellow man is evidence of our love for God.
2. How can God's commandments help us to love our fellow man?
3. In what practical ways should we show the honour due to our parents?
4. Read James 3:8–9 and explain how it is possible to do evil by means of one's tongue.

Lesson 32: (pages 80–81)

The last six commandments:
'You shall not commit adultery'

Questions:
1. Does this commandment refer only to married people?
2. What are the results of the sin of adultery?
3. What is the difference between the sin of adultery and that of theft?
4. What should physical union express?
5. Why is the presence of the Holy Spirit in the heart of the Christian a reason for not indulging in unchastity?

Lesson 33: (pages 81–82)

The last six commandments:
'You shall not steal'
'You shall not bear false witness against your neighbour'
'You shall not covet ...'

Questions:
1. Explain why we must respect that which belongs to our neighbour.
2. Why is bearing false witness in opposition to love for one's fellow man?
3. How can a simple identity card or any official paper constitute a false testimony?
4. Show how covetousness is at the root of all sin.

Chapter 17 The Christian and material things

Lesson 34: (pages 83–84)

Beware of the trap!
God looks after His children
Serving God first

Questions:
1. Is it necessary to be rich, for material things to become a snare?

2. Does a Christian have to be poor or to despise material things?
3. What should be the prime concern of a Christian?
4. How can a Christian use the material things which he possesses to show his love for God and his fellow man?

Chapter 18 The Christian and the world

Lesson 35: (pages 85–86)

What is the world?
God's creation
The enemy of God

Questions:
1. Is the creation of God completely corrupted by sin?
2. Are work and studying included in the service of God? If so, why?
3. In which sense should the Christian not love the world?
4. What are the two dangers which the disciples of Jesus Christ must avoid in the world which is the enemy of God?

Lesson 36: (pages 86–88)

Christian liberty
Sin is not in objects
Above all, let us beware of judging others

Questions:
1. Does Christian liberty give us the right to do anything we like?
2. For whom should we use this liberty?
3. How can covetousness be aroused by the use of legitimate things?
4. Must all Christians abstain from the same things?
5. Would it be right to draw up a list of things which are permitted and forbidden to the Christian?

Chapter 19 The Christian and the state

Lesson 37: (pages 89–90)

The dual nationality of the Christian
The existence of the state is intended by God
Respect due to authorities
The limits of obedience due to the authorities

Questions:
1. Why should the Christian be a loyal citizen of his country?
2. Who instituted the state?
3. Why should the Christian submit to the established authorities?
4. In what circumstances could a Christian have to refuse to obey the authorities?

Lesson 38: (pages 90–92)

Prayer for the authorities
The Christian should take an interest in the affairs of his nation
The Christian and politics
Church leaders and politics

Questions:
1. In what way should a Christian take an interest in the affairs of his nation?
2. What condition must a political party fulfil, if a Christian is to be a member of it?
3. Why should a pastor not accept political responsibility?
4. What are the respective roles of the church and the state in the world?

Chapter 20 The Christian and the local church

Lesson 39: (pages 93–95)

The local church is an embassy
Participation in the life of the local church
The responsibilities of the Christian in the church
The collection

Questions:
1. Why does the local church meet together?
2. What happens to the Christian who neglects to take part in the life of the local church?
3. Do all Christians have the same responsibilities in the local church?
4. Explain how contributing to the collection is not so much a duty as a privilege.

Lesson 40: (pages 95–98)

Discipline
How to practise discipline
Returning to the Lord's Table and taking up responsibilities again

Questions:
1. For what reasons is the exercise of discipline necessary?
2. Why is discipline never a punishment?
3. Compare the method of proceeding taught by Jesus in Matthew 18:15–17 with the customs of the world. What differences can you find?
4. What condition must a Christian, who has fallen, fulfil in order to take his place in the local church again?

Lesson 41: (page 98)

Offices in the local church

Questions:
1. Why are different offices necessary in the local church?
2. What does the word 'office' mean?
3. Read Titus 1:5–9 and enumerate the qualities required in a servant of God?
4. Why are there so few young men and women who go into full-time service for God?